GW00793024

The Yellow Nib

No 11 Spring 2016

Edited by

Leontia Flynn
Frank Ormsby

The Yellow Nib
Edited by Leontia Flynn and Frank Ormsby.

Editorial Board:
Fran Brearton
Edna Longley
Peter McDonald
David Wheatley

Editorial Assistants:
Caitlin Newby
Martin Cromie

Printed by:
CDS

Typeset by:
Stephen Connolly

Subscriptions:
Gerry Hellawell
The Seamus Heaney Centre for Poetry
School of English
Queen's University Belfast
Belfast BT7 1NN
Northern Ireland

www.theyellownib.com

Subscription Rates
£10/€12 per year, for two issues (Great Britain & Ireland)
€20/$25 per year (rest of world)
Plus P&P

Back Issues
Numbers 1 – 5 and number 7 are available.
£5/€6 per back issue (Great Britain & Ireland)
€10/$15 per back issue (rest of world)
Plus P&P

ISBN 978-1-909131-37- 8
ISSN 1745-9621

Contents

REVIEWS

HANNAH LOWE

Four poems

If You Believe: One Pale Eye

If you believe I met Chan Canasta in 1962
after hours in the cold at the stage door,
Canasta sweeping through in his long black coat
as I called out *Sir? Sir?* and he turned
and loomed above me like a vampire,
you may as well believe any of the things
I dream about, watching his old TV shows –
the way he handled a deck of cards up close
(they couldn't catch it with the camera)
like pulling a silk scarf through his fingers,
or the Slavic ghost in his voice, conducting
his guests to pick a card, or think of a card
but *please ladies and gentlemen, keep it secret*
or how he held them all in the corner
of one pale eye, and you knew somehow
he had read their minds. You may as well believe
that night we walked down by the canal
was the first of many times – the narrow boats
in their carnival colours moored in the mist,
the smell of tar, and Chan not looking at me
but talking, talking, as though I was the first person
to ever ask him – of the family in Cracow
lost in the war, of the shaded roof garden
in Jerusalem where he had read book
after book on occultism and mesmerism
and practised his experiments –
if you have talent you must polish it until it glitters
and how he remade himself in Britain –
pilot, magician, English-Polish gentleman.
Was it the first light coming up
brought silence? We sat by the lock,

Chan pulling his cards from his pocket
and holding each one up to his lighter
until the flame spread and the symbols
and faces cindered, and he flung them out
across the dark still water, like firebirds.

HANNAH LOWE

If You Believe: Old Paradise Street

If you believe I played with Phil Seamen in 1970,
a Sunday night, the Dog and Bone half empty,
Phil just keeping time with his sticks in one hand
and then, when the punters flocked in,
his hands a blur on the ghost notes and flams,
you may as well believe anything I dream of
looking at his old album covers –
how on the bus to gigs he'd beat a Yoruba groove
on his knees, or mine, while the passengers stared,
one knee the high-hat, one the snare
or how we drank the night down in the flat
on Old Paradise Street, his record player
spinning through Ghana, through Cuba, Phil
just tapping his feet or later, a fag spilt
from his half-moon heroine grin:
Don't you know at midnight I turn into a pumpkin?
Rack-thin in his old cardigan, drooped
in his chair, but what he knew about drumming
was like opening the door to let sunshine in.
Or you might as well believe that last try
at getting clean, stood on the Burton canal
with his fishing pole or strolling the streets
where the boy he'd been had thrown
the windows wide and whacked his drums
over the backyards and washing lines,
had nearly set him right – 'Phil's Renaissance'
Melody Maker said of the gigs we played
if you could sugar-coat the sweats and sores, the sick.
Who'd guess a nap in his chair would be
the good long sleep? Worn heart, barbiturate-weak.
Goodnight Phil. There's a bright moon tonight
on Waterloo, and the hiss of vinyl on your turntable
spinning spinning the long night through –

HANNAH LOWE

Out of Many

That evening, I was Miss Mahogany,
between Miss Satinwood, Miss Ebony –
parading on the stage before the crowd,
my bust and waist and hip size read aloud,
skin polished as the venue's furniture –
old Bloomfield House, where May, my grandmother,
an octoroon, once scurried from her Master,
so close in looks, he must have been her brother!

Earlier we'd been gauged by tape measure
and shade chart, organised by skin colour.
Now that black was "in" and beautiful
(no more of counting teeth or mapping skulls)
we darker girls in tropical bikinis
could join our paler friends. Miss Ebony,
in every photograph, bookends the row,
the darkest band of colour in our rainbow

shimmering on stage. A shame we three
of darker hues were named for sturdy trees
whereas our lighter sisters down the line
were fruit and blooms: half-way along, Miss Jasmine
and Miss Lotus Flower (Hakka grand-daughters
of Lowe and Chan, indentured labourers)
and smiling at the end, Miss Apple Blossom,
her golden hair arranged on pallid bosom.

The final round saw all the lovely Misses
sashay and twirl in satin ball dresses
and crowns of orchids – none of us exotic
as Miss All-Spice, her hennaed fingers beaked
like birds of paradise, a waft of perfume
as she danced. Then, in the bright-lit dressing room
we scraped the sticky make-up from our faces,
still in line, of course. We knew our places.

HANNAH LOWE

Eleven O'clock Child

Ship Yit Tiam

I said *half caste* at school
before *half caste* was banned
and the next words came in

It's just a little heckle in the yard
Still love you, mule-child
mongrel of the shopkeeper and cook

I was never half anything
just running the asphalt with my friends
bloody knees and hands

Eleven o'clock child
you're not quite noon
not midnight

saving money in a jar
buried on the field
to fly away to America

stuck before
the clock's hands
reached the top

didn't know about one drop rule
counting teeth, hexadecaroon
marrano, mestizo

don't mean you
can't do maths
keep books

Dad said his father called him
ship yit tiam
eleven o'clock child

It's nothing
but a kink of hair
a lip poke

I thought it was kind
not another way
to say unclean

look of skin
cooked too long
not quite clean

PETER MC DONALD

Herne the Hunter

1

With everything wrong, no right way to behave –
even so, this was the worst I could devise:
brutal, when it might have been otherwise.
Are you supposed to take that to the grave?

Once you can bear to look, you see a grove
of elm and ash, where great gashes, the size
of open fists are cut, and the bark lies
in strips and ribbons everywhere:
                              to save
anything now from all the fury and pain
seems barely possible, and such unmeant
gouging and shredding, more or less insane,
that made this carnage just to find some ease
is no worse than we knew, watching the trees
stand still to take their unjust punishment.

2

Is it alive, or not? It is alive,
but threadbare and scooped-looking now, for all
that it succeeds in standing proud and tall,
this cedar, whose old upper boughs contrive
nest-platforms when the building birds arrive,
but not today: today, when a wet squall
strikes the poor man up there, and makes him fall
down through the brittle wood in a high dive.

Is he dead on impact, cut raw, or lamed
when he smacks the forest floor like a bag of bones?
We cannot know, because he never lands,
having slipped long since from the tree's hands,
and stepped out of the air to soil and stones
where the stricken cedar is, tall and ashamed.

3

In the end, there was nothing that I denied;
spelling out guilt like a bad alphabet
in fear, without remorse, I simply let
words lose themselves in the quick tears I cried.

To tap a pine, you cut into its side
through bark and into flesh, into the wet
flesh, where now little v-shapes are set
like signs, carved neatly from narrow to wide
all round the trunk; and there, to catch the new
resin, plastic half-cups and trays are taped.

It comes so slowly you don't see it come
at first, the sticky gradual pine-gum,
like blood that drops and hardens once it's tapped,
or downward-crawling tears that you see through.

4

She stood above him on the moving stairs
and looked around, and smiled, and held his gaze
so that time seemed to stop, go out of phase
with life before and after: unawares,
he stepped up to a height of flashes, flares,
split-second beacons whose strength could amaze
them both together, and leave them in a daze,
pale at a whole world so suddenly theirs.

This was the fullness of a chestnut tree
bursting with lights, dwarfing the two of them;
its blossoms the same colour as the silk
against her skin; its breath enormous, free;
each thousandth leaf held fast on a new stem:
next day, the cows gave blood instead of milk.

5

The trees take shape, and blur their shapes in spring
with white and pink, as random shots of bloom
come everywhere at once with flounce and plume
of excess show, puffing a bright ring
out in a rising circle, that can bring
its fuzzy glare to dead space, fill a room
with erotic, all-imaginary perfume:
the cherry- and the plum-trees blossoming.

Love-poets ought to write with a quill pen
for her alone, or readers in close pairs,
and not for blowsy sorrows of their own;
May gives a tree more light than the tree bears,
unpicking it until the flowers are blown,
while lovers hasten seriously upstairs.

6

From this distance, the birch saplings engrave
thin lines of grey on lighter grey, embrace
each other, tangle, and so interlace
their own likenesses, where they seem to wave
stiffly in the wind.

       Today, when I shave,
I watch my face become my father's face:
he was the better man.

       Whatever trace
there is – if there is anything left, save
these low trees, far away and vulnerable –
to stand in for first things, a few half-bright
resemblances, glowing, ready to pall,
that come and go into and out of sight,
will figure there, just about visible
as birch-bark mirrors the blank early light.

7

Hawthorn to heal the heart: beneath an arc
of blossom, fizzing as it jumps and jigs
with every gust, how many jaggy sprigs
would you need to cut away from leaves and bark
for that medicine to work?

       I see a mark
on each leg, where the sharp cord snaps and digs
at your skin, and lines etched there like twigs
that touch each other gently in the dark.

Thorn runs under the tiny flowers, and faces
upwards beneath them, where you wouldn't see
as you close a hand, then in a dozen places
it leaves its little wounds, intricately
arranged in salmon-and-black corsetry
with hooks and eyes, and buttons and tight laces.

8

And sometimes real tears without warning come,
as if grief could please itself, and these dry
eyes could not take in the tan-yellowy
hazel switches across them without some
working of sudden sorrow, sorrow dumb
about its reasons, but still tuning a cry
past hearing, and pitching itself so high
that leaves and bending wood vibrate and thrum.

I am speaking with the accents of the dead
 – my dead, I mean – whose voices are entwined
with mine, and break apart inside my head
then fade to almost nothing here, behind
my speech and breath when, just over what's said,
I hear a cry of spirits, faint and blind.

9

This last knock split it open, the maple wood
solid until it's broken, only then
coming apart slowly along the grain,
not as strong as it's heavy, and though good
for many things, not for this.
                              Whatever should
have happened, didn't: ten or a dozen men
couldn't budge me, get me loose, or unpen
me from the narrow cage in which I stood.

That strength was weakness really: a mistake
to leave the timber just as it was found
and try to use it, then to watch it break
as it must – as the maples all around
would break in the end, having to forsake
their inward fibres, hard and seldom sound.

10

The patch of mud and moss we called the green,
where footballs whacked and skidded half the day
from children sent out of the house to play,
had three young beeches, each behind a screen
of staked wire netting: as we ran between
them, frantic, we would pull the wire away
on each sharp turn, making them jerk and sway
to kicks and pulls, letting them drag and lean.

Too damaged over months, the trees gave up,
their short lives hurt past bearing. Nothing brings
them back, not even this; and not the look
of them dying, the look of broken things;
but noise after them carried, didn't stop:
frail cages sounded like chains as they shook.

11

Rain-water and the water from the stream
coat shelves of stone, where willow-shadows break
up into abstract cuts of light and dark
the greys and green-greys: nothing is the same
for more than seconds, as the waters teem
down and across and down.

                    All for the sake
of love – really – its well sewn-in mistake
ripped out, a stitched heart torn along the seam;
all for just that, and the threads brushed away.

I can't make out a pattern. Where they sway
with higher winds, the willow branches tilt
downwards and tangle, disordered in the pelt
of rain, and each leaf twists a different way
across limestone that water wants to melt.

12

I kept on seeing the very same oak tree
blasted; sometimes in dreams; sometimes I saw
it really, worried and ragged and raw,
when I had to picture it incessantly
not to see other things, and not to be
taken apart myself, as though the paw
of some black beast had put claw after claw
on to my skin, opened me as a key
opens a lock.

     And what there was to find
was only this: a mess of nerves and blood;
flesh that was going to die anyway
rooted in soil and loam, gravel and mud;
in love doubtless with what it leaves behind;
not saying to the end what it would never say.

CAROL RUMENS

Four Poems

Happy Christmas, Sister Dympna

"Animals *are* people!" Sister Dympna feeds the camera
that twinkly look she got through being chosen
from all the whining, wagging, weaving strays in the enclosure
to be Love's Guide-Dog and the Nation's anchor.
She can't keep cats. Or terrapins. They're people
and she's reserved for God. A venial sin, you say,
this heresy, but what does Pope Francis say?
Has God agreed to a new species-steeple?

Animals don't have souls. Horns, hooves, et cetera,
aren't suited to the sacred menagerie.
No pets, no God, I thought. I had a hamster
I loved and taught some tricks and challenges,
claiming her (airborne in a basket) First
Hamster into Space. And when she died
(in bed and full of hamster-years) I cried.
I'd been a little beast; my skin was fur, reversed.

In those days, mice could sew, dogs dance, and fuchsia piglets
with hats and ginghamed picnic-tables perved
our childhood dream of childhood. Animaddictive,
Tom was an evil psycho, and deserved
to be cat-pancakes. Dragons less than furry,
grinned *ranckes of yron teethe*, burned fossil fuel, and crunched
Anglicans, till we charmed them. Then, like us, they lunched
on salad, muttering "Hurry, oysters, hurry!"

Sister Dympna prays for the word-lords who engrave
small discs with "Dots-Toyevsky", "Mopsy-Mow"
or "Prince". In her new series, *Boss and Slave*
(the Christmas special, *Hoping it Might Be So*),

she steals the keys to all the Pets-at-Home
cages, and – is she dreaming? – whispers, "Run,"
before she kneels, on cue, and finds the new-born Son
curled in his hay, blind as a kitten, bless Him.

CAROL RUMENS

A Few Study-Notes

"Stone walls do not a prison make,
Nor iron bars a cage:
Minds innocent and quiet take
That for an hermitage".

(Richard Lovelace, 'To Althea, from Prison')

1.

I couldn't sleep. I'd got back late from the Ministry,
bruised by linen-board and letterpress –

old, heavy, a gourmet meal, prepared for no-one
(a tenant child, perhaps, an errant husband),

sure to congeal unhappily and revolt
microbially. I went outside. The moon

was lost, the clouds like half-cooked Yorkshire pudding.

*

The full blaze was a double chrysanthemum
I'd never seen before, mottled with blackfly.

Pulsating, blood-supplied, it was the mirror image
of an uncorrected lens. I leave it uncorrected

since everyone knows what the full moon looks like.

*

The wind was cool, then cold as scholarship.
The lamps stood unconfined in various bivouacs.

I drank some year-old grapes, and turned to you, my four-
centuries-old convicted Royalist.

Richard, your lines were danceable, but burned me –
that footnote like a detached retina.

I sleepily revolved the aesthetic question
but couldn't solve it: is it "gods" or "birds"

that wanton in your hand? I wonder what you hear
in Althea's hair-thin whispers through the trickle

of sewage, rain and rust. Outside, there's war,
England's blown chrysanthemum, riven with gods and birds.

2.

At the Ministry, I'd found a plastic out-tray
had replaced my wooden nest-box –

Now with a different, younger name on it,
other white eggs inside it.

What are you trying to tell me, Minister?

What was my nest-box, anyway, but a cuckoo?

*

The prefecture, some four li north of here,
has pizzerias and happy hours and nail-bars,

and stacks of broiler-boxes. New translators
work on the tongue of this year's press release.

The Prefect-Scribbler writes, *You will enjoy the mountains.
Here*, we feel free. His eloquence delights him.

Sing, O gods and birds, sing, dying muses,
the new illiteracy of imagination.

*

When the migrant young fly in, the Ministry
pats its hard pockets. *I, too, like to eat.*

Hatred sizzles across my paths like bush-fire.
I stamp it down: opaline ash-curls, flight-feathers.

The Prefect grabs at the phoenix, almost strangles it.
He has no blaze, no neck and an eternal smile.

3.

Wind in the silence. Words. I sometimes meet them.
They never begin by asking for a light,

never return a text: they chew their lips
like stubborn children who confide their day

only if you desist from questioning them,
or else keep up a stare

so long you see the first pond-water eye
hair-pricked by sunbeams, pinned until it seeps

a retinal cell, and another retinal cell
and what it sees would have been called "amazing"

if any mouth had formed, or any mouthing.
When word-suns shine, it's not philosophy.

*

In the eggshell dawn, the courtier climbs alone,
takes No-Guide Path, and Hard Way

and Ankle-Twist path and Downhill and Re-Track,
and sleeps in the common tanning salon, pillowed

on quartz. He has no Personal Development Plan.
By the King's humility, and the poet's *cyfieithiad*

of stone and iron, his lamp is fed and lighted.
Flutter of doodled cupids, escaped birds ...

Fly, dear Richard, footloose Cavalier.

His dance-steps fade in cloud-wisps, maiden-hair.

(Note: cyfieithiad (Welsh)– translation)

CAROL RUMENS

In Memory of a Rationalist

A man lies dressing-gowned among his arguments,
dying, pitiless. His head feels small
and analogue, unlike the instruments
which live his life, now, with a sad lack of style

or appetite. On digits, thoughts depend –
a circuitry they find profoundly facile.
Sparing his friends the presence of a mind
Un-catheterised, he schemes to shake that muscle.

He picks his question (answerless, in the end)
and waits. Not like old songs, but sharp as gods they come
Explication, Comparison, Example,

Exhortation – Olympian athletes all,
sparring through morphine's bland encomium
as he yells praise and insults from the trainer's stand.

CAROL RUMENS

Hamlet

freely after Boris Pasternak

The noise died. I stepped onto the stage.
And now I lean against a door-frame, tense,
Straining to hear the drama of events
Interpreting the drama of our age.

The deepening dusk's thousand binoculars
Take aim at me, point-blank along the one
Axis. Not a blink. If it can be done,
Father, Abba, I beg – *let my cup pass.*

I love your bloody plots! I'd willingly
Take any part you offered me, but this –
The part you're writing now. The scenes unfold

As planned, the actors stride their entrances.
And I'm alone, trumped by the Pharisee.
"To live a life is not to cross a field."

JOHN REDMOND

The Big Freeze

Quirky how
you want to hear my horse-laugh.
Distantly, we download
a space-photograph
of Britannia
frozen to her broomstick.
At either end of it
we're stuck.

The level of falling is set to continue.
 "When did Scooby Doo
enter our relationship?"
From their window below
'our' dopeheads bestow
yellow-dark gobs
on the slush.
 "Was it after Sebadoh?"

"You got them on in the background?"
"Hey, we're slackers (cough) ... I suppose."
"No. We're slobs."
Spotified lo-fi
fizzles down the aromatic stairwell.
"Chicken, do you want me to become a Catholic?"
Into my slovenly Nokia I neigh.

OLIVER MORT

Painting in the Abstract

We arrive in B&Q like Picasso
or van Gogh

Ready to buy tubs of Crown paint
for the blank canvas

Of our newly bought "Victorian"
Belfast townhouse

Which will be painted in six days
of utter madness

And yet we are not Picasso
or van Gogh

I will not cut my ear off or you
end up in an asylum

Our brushes and rollers will not
create a masterpiece

To be hung in some museum, our
insanity studied in silence

We will instead lay down old curtains
and masking-tape the edges

And carefully brush and roll all our future
wonder and suffer

And laughs and screams and
crack ups

And breakdowns into the perfect
combination of colour

OWEN GALLAGHER

We Are Closing In Five Minutes!

Leave me in a public library
    with floor-to-ceiling wooden shelves,
        rows and rows of little alleyways

where I can wrestle with thinkers,
    brush against painters,
        and roam through fields of poems,

then take a vacation in the travel section
    or ski down slopes of the world wide web
        to land amongst picture books

where I feel like Gulliver
    as I step over tiny tots
        who carpet the floor and yell

to their parents; 'Again! Once more!'
    where keyless kids sit alongside
        those doing essays or a hundred lines,

or are too afraid to go home,
    and those in search of a fix
        of print, or a daytime abode.

I make for the 'New Arrivals,'
    and place myself under house-arrest
        until the librarian's voice booms.

BYRON BEYNON

Two Poems

A Corner of the Artist's Room in Paris (with Open Window)

after the painting by Gwen John

She is isolated
within her room,
its open window
an eye onto the mysterious sky.
She is there watching
with us,
new-lighted,
as we see a coat
discarded on a chair
delicate as lace.
Her shy table
up against the wall
keeps company
with an anonymous book,
its leaves exposed
to the subtle strokes of moon and air.
A determined silence waits.

BYRON BENYON

Coleridge on Scafell

He speaks his mind
in a Devonshire accent,
leaves home on a Sunday
morning for nine days
to walk around the Lake District.
He disregards the weather,
has no professional guide,
his thoughts high
on fresh air,
freedom and adventure.
He sees the wild, green panorama,
a sunset viewed from the sheepfold
with dreams for company.
A letter written on Scafell,
bruised ink on paper,
the thundery forecast
in a life,
with those clouds
that came from the sea.

FAYE BOLAND

Miss Marple

Miss Marple,
buttoned up
black-bereted,
stop-starts
her bubble car
on the narrow lane,
forgets to indicate
as she joins
the main road,
slows-up traffic,
forced to overtake.
Mounts the kerb
as she parks,
rear end jutting out
into a long stream
of swerving vehicles
ignores
the double yellows
beneath her

ELIZABETH BARRETT

Two Poems

Foundling

The mothers left printed birds
and acorns, butterflies and flowers
on cuffs of cherryderry and lawn,
flannel and linsey torn from their petticoats.
A ribbon or piece of gown was bound
into a billet book for the foundling child;
one woman stitched her son's initials
in red worsted on this frayed swatch.

If you could match the piece
you could reclaim your child.
I imagine a mother burying half
a camblet heart in a drawer
or tacking a scrap of paduasoy silk
into the lining of her bra.

There is no ledger for my token;
nowhere to record my daughter's
distinguishing marks or the clothes
she was wearing when last I saw her
(purple converse, denim jeans, a mole
on her abdomen, scar on her left knee).

Like a foundling mother I rummage
through off-cuts: in my sewing box
I find her name stitched in green
on cream cotton tape; a silver butterfly
snipped from a purse; her first stitches
in red aida. I choose a calico ribbon
embroidered with cornflowers: fold and cut
it at the crease; slip half under my pillow.

ELIZABETH BARRETT

My Daughter Falling

Another Christmas without her.
I walk Limb Valley to the meadow,
winter feed scattered in the fields,
sheep wandering among mangel roots.
In my silent pocket the blue balloons
of unanswered texts on my phone.

I'm wearing the boots I bought her,
can feel blood between my toes.
At the bog I slip on the crossing-stones –
remember how she fell a third time
here that day: I don't understand,
I'd said to her, why you are always falling.

The first time, I opened the door
to find her there. I could hardly look
at the blood and her knee flapping
open, exposing muscle and bone.
She'd been running home to me,
she told me – rushing to get home.

The second time was in the snow.
She re-split her knee, opened it
exactly as before; another chance for me
to scoop my daughter in my arms,
rush her to be cleaned and stitched.
How, again, I'd failed at this.

Was that why she slipped and fell
on these crossing-stones that day?
A last test. I couldn't re-balance
her; didn't help her to her feet. Instead
I'd said, despairing: I don't understand
why you are always falling.

My final response to my daughter falling
was this pair of North Face boots.
She left them to me when she went.
Her size. Now I'm the one losing
my balance, slipping like a child.
No one to pick me up. A mother falling.

Some details in 'Foundling' are based on records kept by the London Foundling Hospital 1741-1760

KEVIN QUINN

Two Poems

Boat Shed

The pliancy of larch
fed length by length

through the steam box
in Corrigan's lean-to shed

and bent, still sappy,
to the curvature

of a keel my quiet father's
planing, sanding down,

painting coat after coat
that trademark blue

the Reids, the Boyds
will blazon summer

on summer now
the length and breadth

of the lough,
staying away all day,

the islands to themselves,
slipping back in the dark

to the shore, the unlit streets,
juggling the oar-locks,

leaving back the oars.

KEVIN QUINN

Mercers' Window

That side of High Street
gets the sun early

and the threadbare awning's
no help to the shop girl

reaching blind into
Mercers' window

past brooches, bracelets,
Belleek, to reach,

right at the back,
in its velveteen pouch,

the new slimline Parker,
its chevronned top

a promise of fluency, ease
has beckoned all summer

to scholarship boys
will be leaving soon

for lodgings, digs,
whose addresses

they rehearse, repeat,
on the fly-leaves of

textbooks, primers.
The ink dries to an uncertain blue

on the tall leafless avenues,
Wellesley, Fitzroy, Dunluce

ELAINE GASTON

Two Poems

The Wood from the Trees

The big ash tree blew down in the paddock.
First George buzzed it up with the chain saw,
then split each length again with the axe.
We filled turf bags, animal feed bags,
loaded the trailer up and drove to my house
where they are stacked in my porch.

Some logs are forked, some dry, some damp.

Some, from the north side of the tree,
are big rough hunks covered in lichen.
Some are split exactly right.
One is so big it will not fit in the grate.
I have to wait until half of it burns,
then push the other half in.

I can almost see the exact branch each block came from.

Their vetiver smell covers my clothes, my hair.
My front is roasted, my back always cold.
They click and shift in the hearth
as a snag of moss or a cobweb catches.
The blaze flares up. Flame spurts through a Y,
roars out an O.

Some are still in the green, will not take.

Those ones need plenty of coal at the base
to burn well with the Planters' beech
and the last Bord na Móna briquette.
All mixed together, they are the bright,
hard, firm, basis of my fire—
my vowels, my consonants, my definite articles.

ELAINE GASTON

The Dark Hedges

Jamesy was walking back from the dole one day
down The Hedges. It was about 3 miles home.
Better wearing out the boots
than wearing out the bedclothes,
his father had barked at him.

At the time you had to sign on in the Orange Hall
— imagine! — the wooden floor, sun and dust smell,
mahogany boxes with yellow cards.
A desk, a chair, a file of people
queued out the door.

He was scunnered in the cold, early morning.
On the way back he snapped
a few photos with his second-hand camera.
The local paper published one. Everyone wanted it.
The corner shop made it into a black and white postcard.

Then the negative got scratched, the original got lost,
and he went across the water
with his camera and a folder full of photos.
He traipsed round everywhere to find work.
This was long before film sets or tourist buses back here.

On the day of the ceasefire
a big London broadsheet newspaper
ran an article and a full-page feature
of his photo — The Dark Hedges
as first light filtered through the inky branches.

RUTH CARR

from 'Feather and Bone'

On

knot the ribbon
twin loops, not single
fingers find the tear in the veil

your sister stitched together
ripped by a guardsman's sword
in the throng

before
your brother rose to the occasion of his hanging
accepted the rope like a garland round his neck

an hour ago it seems

the heavy door feels heavier
pause on the threshold
listening for something

the same Rosemary Lane with sparrows cheeping
the world at its business
nothing – everything – nothing

has altered

force your feet down the entry –
a harmless handcart
rattles right through you

stopping your breath as you see there again
in its splintered arms
the cooling corpse

that housed the lungs, dear head
the heart
you could not waken

your own beats hard in its slender cage
on you go
without flinching

Mary Ann's Reconcilliation Sheet

Reckoned the cost of every thing
oxtail, oats, ham bones for soup
strings for a harp, a bed for Atty
the cost of his sweets and music paper
the cost of counting on neighbours
of ribbon, chambric, flour sacks, the coach
to Dublin, the cost of the lash on the backs
of the horses, muslin in purest white
for the jailor's wife, the lifelong gift
of a sister's hand – her craft, your figures
your running, her calm, the cost of keeping going
supplying demand, feeding mouths –
outspinners', weavers' kin, the gain
of open arms to take his Maria in –
the insurmountable price of a brother's life –
the grief not ending there
the starving line of love
        one by one

you drew a line through pity
knew the score of the quill
embarrassed committees beyond their natural mean
realised in soap and sheets and lime
the right to be clean in the bowels of charity
behind those stately walls

        ninety six years
reconciling loss to incremental gain

Just

And did you sometimes want to leave if off ?
pack it back in the box ?
return it there, where your mother's milliners' hands
picked the first one out for you ?

just to be
back up Cave Hill on horseback,
Harry beside you, debating the Rights of Woman
listening, lamenting, laying down the law
your big visions drawing you on
looking out on the Lough and Carrickfergus
not knowing the way things would go
just throw your head back and laugh
the Northerly wind in your hair and letting it blow

Note: These poems are part of a book-length exploration of the lives of Mary Ann McCracken and Dorothy Wordsworth, whose lives ran parallel with one another but never crossed. 'On' focuses on the execution of Henry Joy McCracken as a leader of the 1798 Rebellion, and the impact this had on his sister. 'Mary Ann McCracken's Reconciliation Sheet' attempts to draw up the losses and gains of her life.

'Atty' refers to Edward Bunting, who could not have completed an archive of Irish Harp Music without the support of the McCracken family.

Enda Coyle Greene

Friday, Saturday, Sunday, City

Friday

finds us closer
to strangers,

only inches away
beyond thin glass,

gone as soon
as they arrive

on the pavement
in their own strange lives.

Saturday

could be spent just meeting ourselves
as flickers in shop windows,

but we lose the afternoon
to a gallery, to all those faces

faced with an amalgam
that's as complex or as simple

as our conversation later,
in the brittle glint spring.

Sunday

we close the door behind us
on last orders

and that girl drinking with a man
who's pretending to be drunk.

While you hail a taxi in the rain,
I'll be driven away,

looking out at you through glass
the wipers won't quite dry.

ERIKA MEITNER

Three Poems

Gun Show Loophole

I don't know what Anna and I hope to find
at the Salem gun show, but before we go
we read "101 Gun Show Tips." Number 26:
bring a small dolly—ammo is heavy. Number 30:
have identification ready—99 percent of the time
you will be asked to provide a government-issued
ID when purchasing a firearm.

What about the other one percent, says Anna,
pointing out the obvious loophole. If you Google
'gun show loophole' the word "loophole" often
appears in quotes next to the phrase 'infringing
on Second Amendment rights.' At the gun show,
there are no photos, no recordings, no reporters' notes
allowed. At the gun show, men carry guns that are
presumably not loaded because a sign says DO NOT
BRING LOADED GUNS INTO THE BUILDING.

Men enter with hunting rifles and semi-automatic
weapons slung over their shoulders, pistols in belt
holsters, sometimes both. They are, as the saying
goes, armed to the teeth, but no one at the gun show
smiles. Not the guy at the Friends of the NRA booth
whose name is actually Smiley and tells us women
have a sixth sense, make great shots once we get over
our fear of weapons—something about our heart rates—

nor the Ben Carson for President table staffers who sit
across from a booth of Confederate flag paraphernalia;
Kiss My Rebel Ass and The South Will Rise Again tank
tops don't seem as bad as the crimson and black Nazi

memorabilia, though the guy running that booth looks
hipster rather than terrifying, which is how the man
selling bone-handled knives looks: bearded survivalist
hunkered down behind his merchandise, each blade
perched in its antlered display stand. He would gut me
in a heartbeat.

This poem has traveled from place to place crumpled
in my purse, in a notebook, on receipts. It comes with me
to the hair salon where the bridal party getting their chignons
and loose waves sprayed one more time before the ceremony
discuss the confederate flag scandal at the local high school:
students suspended for protesting a ban by wearing clothes
emblazoned with the stars and bars, their parents driving past
the school with giant flags flapping from the backs
of pickups. I write this poem at baseball practice, sitting

in the shaded dugout at Casey Jones field, where I'm
the only parent without a Southern accent. The dad next to me
is wearing a rebel flag sweatshirt, BATTLE CRY printed
across an airbrushed scene of dogs barking at a raccoon
that's run up a pole to escape them. When the team goes in
for a huddle, they shout *get 'er done* and I'm relieved no one
bows a head to pray to Jesus. I've been living in the South now
for most of my adult life. You shall love your neighbor as yourself,
says Leviticus 19:18 and the word in Hebrew for neighbor
is ray'-ah—masculine for *friend, companion, fellow, other.*

I am neighbor and I am other. I'm a Jew and the white mother
of a black son and a white son. I am trying to understand,
so I listen to the man at a gun show booth telling a small crowd
how he designed a flashlight-taser for blunt-force hits—
to capture hair, skin, DNA in its metal ridges. *You can
keep it in your purse,* he says. *You can keep it in your
glove box, but these are not replacements for your gun,*
he says and points to the .45 on his hip in a holster.

I am trying to understand what to do with the tiny
Rugers and Glocks and Sig Sauers in pink and black,

or purple and black, or pink and purple mottled camo—
the ladies' models—small caliber pieces all heavier
than they look and leashed to tables. I can pick up any gun
I want, weigh it in my palm the way my grandmother
used to measure ingredients for cooking, the way my sons
bring me things they've gathered: pinecones or rocks
or handfuls of wood chips. I have no family history
with fire-arms except as the rounded-up, the looking-down
-the-barrel-of, the guarded-to-prevent-escape.

Here at the Civic Center most booths are family-run
businesses selling pain-salve, first-aid kits, military antiques,
gold-gleaming bullets portioned out in plastic bags. A mom
behind a table displaying scopes and other tactical optics
says *put those shoes back on* to her toddler son, who looks
the same age as my toddler son. I can't bring myself to put
my finger on a trigger—not even the ones on the pink
micro compact carry Beretta that looks like candy.

Snag free design makes it easy to carry reads the text
on the box. *Any gun is better than no gun,* says the Trader
Jerry's salesman. You shall not take vengeance or bear
a grudge against your countrymen—the children
of your people, says Leviticus 19:18:. What kind
of loophole is kinship? And to whom do we feel it?

ERIKA MEITNER

HolyMoleyLand

In *The Odyssey* there's mention of a plant called moly, which is sacred and harvested only by the gods.

The gods are vengeful but they are also good to us, though we have given up sacrifices and burnt offerings.

With regard to burnt offerings, the following is a concise statement of the Levitical law: these were wholly animal, and the victims were wholly consumed.

The Animal Gang was a marauding group of hooligans who used potatoes studded with razor blades during pitched battles on the streets of Dublin in the 1930s.

Which is to say that the moley was an ordinary potato, its surface jagged with metal edges.

"Holy moley!" was Captain Marvel's characteristic exclamation of surprise.

Because the oath might have been offensive to some, "Holy moly" was used in the late 1920s as a jocular euphemism for "Holy Moses."

Holy Moses is also a German thrash metal band, known for its lead singer Sabina Classen—one of the first and only women to use a death growl.

Moses demanded the release of the Israelites from slavery, and led them out of Egypt and across the Red Sea. After 40 years of wandering in the desert, he died within sight of the promised land.

In *A Dictionary of the Underworld*, 'moley' is preceeded by 'mokker'— the Yiddish word for maker.

'Mokker' is a variation of 'macher,' which also means someone who arranges, fixes, or has connections. The man who could miraculously produce a visa or get an exit permit for a Jew was known as a 'macher.'

The story in *The Guardian* of an Austrian Jewish shepherd who drives Syrian refugees across southern Hungary to eastern Austria, hidden under blankets in his car—*All my shoes got torn to pieces at the Hungaaaaaarian border*, he sings, to the tune of a Jewish wedding song, to cheer everyone in his vehicle up.

In *Survival in Auschwitz*, Primo Levi writes, "Perhaps 400 yards from the camp lay the potatoes—a treasure. Two extremely long ditches, full of potatoes and covered by alternate layers of soil and straw to protect them from the cold. Nobody would die of hunger any more."

Concerning the unblemished animals from the herd or the flock: The fire which consumed the offerings was never allowed to go out. Every morning the ashes were conveyed by the priest to a clean place outside the camp.

Many boys in the Animal Gang worked as newspaper vendors—a line of employment that would have given them an intimate awareness of the city and its machinations.

In order to transform into Captain Marvel, homeless newsboy Billy Batson spoke the wizard Shazam's name—an acronym for the wisdom of Solomon, the strength of Hercules, the stamina of Atlas, the power of Zeus, the courage of Achilles, and the speed of Mercury. Speaking the word produced a bolt of magic lightning which transformed Billy into Captain Marvel. Speaking the word again reversed the transformation with another bolt of lightning. This is the way some people believe prayer works.

We are frightened, we are frightened by everything, says one of the Syrian refugees, sitting in the darkness. Please can we just keep driving.

Border Song is a gospel ballad first performed by Elton John, with lyrics written by Bernie Taupin—except for the final verse, which John wrote himself: *Holy Moses let us live in peace / Let us strive to find a way to make all hatred cease.*

Captain Marvel battled many villains, including Adolf Hitler's champion Captain Nazi, who was part of The Monster Society of Evil. The Society tried many plans, such as attempting to use Captain Nazi to steal magic fortune-telling pearls, using a film to intimidate the world, and even trying to use a giant cannon to blow holes in countries.

There are holes in all of these stories, our stories—open mouthed gaps in the fence, a singing presence. Holy moley, *please can we just keep driving.*

The phrase "Holy Moley" might have also come from political jingles referencing Professor Raymond Charles Moley, an American economist, and an ally of President Franklin Roosevelt. He served as part of Roosevelt's "Brain Trust" until he turned against the New Deal and became a conservative Republican.

Our entire country's collective genesis: those who were persecuted, who survived, who fled. My mother was stateless until she was six. She still remembers the rocking of the boat. The General Robert Taylor, a converted American troop ship, carried post-war refugees— carried my family—from German Displaced Persons camps to America in 1952.

Conservative Republicans are generally split on how to handle the Syrian refugee crisis. Senator Ted Cruz (R-Texas) indicated he's against the idea of taking in refugees, saying there are logistical and other challenges. Senator Marco Rubio (R-Fla.) has said he's open to the idea of accepting more refugees, as long as security is a top consideration.

Moley wrote the majority of Roosevelt's first inaugural address, but he is not credited with penning the famous line, "the only thing we have to fear is fear itself," though he did write, "only a foolish optimist can deny the dark realities of the moment."

Holy Moses has released the following classic thrash metal albums: "World Chaos," "Terminal Terror," "Too Drunk to Fuck," "Master of Disaster," "Disorder of the Order," and "Agony of Death."

Holy holy holy is the Lord of Hosts. Holy holy holy is the Lord on High.

In 1947 Eleanor Roosevelt visited the D.P. camp at Bergen-Belsen. The story goes that my grandmother, in the crowd, held my mother up high in the air because she wanted Eleanor to see her red-headed child, born from the ashes.

And in his speech celebrating the 70th anniversary of the liberation of Bergen-Belsen, Ronald Lauder, a big macher in the World Jewish Congress said, *when they begged for help, all they got was silence.* And when he said *from the ashes of this terrible place,* he meant the large swath of land known as the Field of Ashes, which stretches behind the gas chambers.

And the priest shall take off his linen garments, and put on other garments, and carry forth the ashes outside the camp unto a clean place.

When a reporter interviewed Aphrodite Vati Mariola, whose family owns the Aphrodite Hotel in Lesbos, about the boats of refugees washing up on the beach, she said: *One boy yesterday, he had with him the Bible written in Arabic. It was from a friend of his and he said he was taking care of it. He just kept crying, bursting into tears. And we kept saying, are you OK? And he said no, no, no – I'm OK, I'm just thanking God that I'm alive.*

In 1933, When Franklin Roosevelt was sworn in he wore a morning coat and striped trousers for the inauguration, and took the oath with his hand on his family Bible, open to I Corinthians 13:

Holy Moly, if I have the gift of prophecy and can fathom all mysteries and all knowledge, and if I have a faith that can move mountains, but do not have love, I am nothing.

There are things I will never know. There are stories that are past telling. No matter how much testimony we gather. No matter how many details we proclaim.

The space between the hole and the holy, the torn passports, desperation and possibility, the exclamation, the slow vanishing of everything including memory.

ERIKA MEITNER

Told on the Mountain

with lines from RaMell Ross's "On South County, Alabama"
and Parashat B'shallah/Exodus 13:17-17:16

The American South as Jerusalem:
a psychic residue that accompanies the air.

Pillar of fire, pillar of cloud—
how to unburden body and skin
from the problem of representation:

strike the rock and water will issue from it;
and there was no water for the people to drink.

I was working from an idea:
to engage the photographic narrative—
to follow that holy light
but provide some breathing room.

Time was physical patience—time
was haptic lull in the deep
South, the historic South and

people may have a change of heart
when they see war, when they return
to Egypt roundabout—by way of the wilderness,

when they exact an oath from their children,
when they carry the bones of their ancestors
up the mountains and loosen the hold

of iconic meaning, utterly blot out
memory, quietly address the function
of skin as it feeds our imagination.

We never exchanged names.

I was working from an idea:
people acknowledge every person
who passes them. Every subconscious

withdrawal in the South of spontaneity
seemed to be traceable to something—

there was the cloud with the darkness
their experience, my experience,
an art that tries to erase the horizon.

NICK LAIRD

Coppa Italia

If I prefer to drink in Irish pubs in non-Irish nations
it's because misquotations are more revealing
and Tino and Patrick are waiting in Whelans

on Via Leonina. The students lounge on the steps
of the fountain drinking Peroni and quoting
themselves as Tommaso locks up the hardware

store and Teresa stares hard at her hands in the three-
wheeled Piaggio Ape they're about to drive home.
The day-old-heat settles down between the buildings

whose upper occupants could shake hands across
the street. Patrick, the catholic, will father five kids
and Tino have so many awful operations on his brain

he'll forget how to read though not how to write.
Edoardo rattles the grille of Gocce di Memoria
down on the painted eyes of the wooden puppets,

and the heat of the sun is stored in the cobble stones
it shone all day on, and we can find nothing sublime
that is not also like this, a transfer of power, a pass.

It is Saturday and late in the desert of the real.
The table I like best is out on the cobbles, a plastic
table of plastic red with a plastic tablecloth

attached to it with metal clips. The laminate
is stamped with the trompe l'oeil of the gaps
and fretwork of a real cast-iron table. Inside,

waiting for the pints to settle, a violence on
the small bright pitch. A man in blue and a man
in a red shirt float, collide, collapse and rise

as one thing turned on itself; are held apart
and talked down and striding back beneath
the floods blue is distraught, a sacker of cities,

but when the camera pans to red he's laughing,
supple and sleek as a stamen at the centre
of a long four-petalled shadow, waiting for

the ball to pollinate him, deep in their half.

In the Endeavour we Translate

Sarah Howe, *Loop of Jade*, Chatto &Windus, £9.99
Andrew McMillan, *Physical*, Jonathan Cape, £9.99

Sarah Howe's first full collection is obsessively concerned with hybridity, heterogeneity, difference, and manifests these themes through a formal restlessness, moving from free verse to sonnet, from stichic to stanzaic forms and from verse to prose with ease. Indeed, many of these modes are displayed within the title poem which explores the poet's relationship with her mother and her Chinese heritage through an almost baroquely skilled collage of folksong, anecdotal prose and verse. The poem begins by describing moments when the poet's mother would speak about her troubled upbringing in China, reflecting on the "pause-pocked, melodic, strangely dated hesitancy" of the mother's speech, before presenting a monologue in the voice of the mother which approximates her vocal idiosyncrasies through well-judged tabulation. When the poem shifts into verse for its final section and returns to the autobiographical voice of the poet, the mother's inheritance is encoded genetically in the disrupted rhythms and syntax as the sentences become choked with commas and dashes: ("I saw that place — / its joss-stick incensed mist, the fortune- / casting herd, / their fluttering, tree-tied pleas — only later / as a tourist".)

Howe's focus on the Chinese side of her heritage could easily lapse into a lazy orientalism and in this regard the presentation of the book does not help; there is an unmistakable air of chinoiserie about the blurb which actually begins "There is a Chinese proverb". The poet however is much too clever and much too aware of both contemporary and historical presentations of China in Western discourse: there is a poem titled 'Chinoiserie' which begins with a tone of half-joking rebuke: "I said *Sleepy Willow*. You said *Voiture*. // That was one of our shorter arguments." The book's epigraph comes from Borges and references "a certain Chinese encyclopaedia" which sorts animals into thirteen absurd categories. These categories are then used as titles for a loose sequence of poems which are interspersed throughout the collection allowing Howe to describe a series of chimeras sometimes literal, sometimes metaphoric, and often textual. In these poems Howe's impressive imagination is allowed to run riot and simultaneously deconstruct stereotypical notions of China through a disjunctive mash-up of allusions and emotional states which often subvert the poems' comic premises with depravity and violence.

Howe is a remarkably good phrase-maker but a handful of the poems are just too pretty. Take for example these lines from the opener 'Mother's Jewellery Box' "a moonlit lake / ghostly lotus leaves / unfurl in tiers"; a kind reading might suggest that this kind of ornate language is entirely appropriate for the thing described, but by the time the poem is over one is left with a sense that nothing much has happened, that perhaps we want the poem to be more than a chain of beautiful words. Moments like this however are very much the exception and usually the surface gorgeousness is there to act as a trojan horse for difficult, disturbing and fascinating ideas; there are not many poetry books this beautiful which also encapsulate emigrant displacement, child abuse, incest and political murder.

Like Howe, Andrew McMillan is a poet who works very much within the lyric tradition. He consciously presents Thom Gunn as an influence in 'Saturday Night', described as a 'broken cento for Thom Gunn'. What this means is that the final line of each quatrain in McMillan's 'Saturday Night' is quoted from Gunn's poem of the same title. It is an experiment which half works: McMillan's description of a sexual encounter in a gay sauna is refreshingly frank in is awkwardness, though when read alongside Gunn's original, one begins to wonder if McMillan has intervened enough on Gunn's poem to justify his own as a new text. But then again maybe this is the point; maybe McMillan's poem is seeking to commune with Gunn's rather than displace it: an erotics, rather than an anxiety of influence.

Much of the reaction to *Physical* has tried to position McMillan as the inheritor to Gunn, but many poems in the book suggest that he has learnt just as much from Mark Doty. We see this most in the short lyrics that comprise the first and third sections of Physical, which are often structured around a three part movement, from observation to description to extrapolation/revelation. When this works, in poems like 'Screen' or 'Urination', we are reminded that even the most traditional of lyric structures have capacity to create genuine surprise. Indeed, 'Urination' may well be the best poem in the book or at least the poem in which McMillan's worship of the male body is able to express the greatest range of emotion. Sometimes however, this tendency towards epiphany results in statements which may sound impressive but do not quite hold up to scrutiny. For example in 'Strongman' when McMillan states "what is masculinity if not taking the weight // of a boy and straining it from oneself" we might be tempted to reply "well, any number of things".

The centrepiece of the book is the long poem 'Protest of the Physical' which had previously been published as a standalone pamphlet. In the poem, McMillan contextualises his erotic encounters with an unnamed man and (again) Thom Gunn within a rangy description of his hometown of Barnsley. For a poem which apparently attempts to tell us something of a place it feels strangely dislocated and impressionistic, at times slipping away into abstraction. However the more securely situated episodes in the poem do seem to accrue an extra subjective importance through their contrast to the surrounding linguistic magma. 'Protest of the Physical' may be taken as a diorama of the book as a whole: at times it could do with a stricter editorial hand to weed out some of the more self-consciously 'poetic' softness, but it also displays McMillan's skill with queer eroticism, and his minute detailing of the male body which is unflinching, yes, but never surgically cold.

PADRAIG REGAN

At The Border Between Languages

Ciaran Carson, *From Elsewhere*, The Gallery Press, €13.90 pbk.

Born into an Irish-speaking household in monoglot, Anglophone Belfast, Ciaran Carson has written of how 'the ghost of Irish' hovers behind his poetry and prose in English. Bilingualism, or rather multilingualism, is the matrix from which Carson's own experiments in language emerge; so it is little wonder that translation has played such an important role in his work, since his first pamphlet, The Insular Celts, appeared in 1973. Besides his book-length translations from the Irish – *The Midnight Court* (2005) and *The Táin* (2007) – he has produced finely-tuned poems translated from Latin, Welsh, Romanian, Japanese, and Italian, including a remarkable version of Dante's *Inferno*. However, for nearly twenty years Carson's most sustained dialogue betwixt and between languages has been with French and the French literary tradition. At times, this dialogue manifests itself in the form of actual translations, such as 1998's The Alexandrine Plan, a suite of poems by Baudelaire, Rimbaud, and Mallarmé rendered into English; or 2012's *In the Light Of*, a verse translation of Rimbaud's *Illuminations*. At others, it is registered by the pervasive Paris-Belfast axis of books such as *For All We Know* (2008) and *Exchange Place* (2012), in which translations between French and English are simply part of the texture of the characters' experience, and contribute to a broader awareness of cultural bi-location. In this expanded sense, translation describes the process of transaction or exchange that occurs between words, idioms, and vocabularies that reveals the difference that is internal to language itself, its fundamental otherness. Or, as Carson has it, 'poetry itself is a kind of translation'.

Carson's latest collection, *From Elsewhere*, translates eighty-one poems from the French of Jean Follain, each of which is accompanied by an 'original' poem that responds to or reworks its counterpart – 'translations of the translations', as Carson describes them in his brief, illuminating introduction. As is customary, the book is meticulously ordered and arranged in three equal sections, each containing fifty-four poems, and beginning and ending with poems that echo one another. The threefold division of the volume recalls the structure employed for his previous books of illness and loss, *On the Night Watch* (2009) and *Until Before After* (2010); whilst Carson himself notes that the format of paired poems is adapted from *For All We Know*. The poems are arranged in sequences that allow the reader to note recurrent images, phrases, and sound patterns, but without insisting upon any kind of continuous narrative thread.

Follain was born in 1903 in Canisy, Normandy and spent most of his adult life as a lawyer and magistrate. Although he lived for many years in central Paris, his poems often recall the rural landscapes and kitchen interiors of his childhood, employing an eye for concrete details and exactly-defined images that recalls the pictorial realism of painters such as Chardin or Millet. Many of the poems that Carson chooses to translate are also shadowed by the after-effects of the European wars, inflecting domestic or bucolic scenes with an air of indefinable menace that occasionally borders on the surreal. For instance, in 'Unsoir se refait: Reprise', evening falls on a village scene after some unspecified act of violence, and the short poem ends:

> a beast slouches to its corner
> untroubled by the days of horror
> which reprise a couple
> at the turning of a road
> swamped with birds.

Carson introduces deliberate echoes of Yeats and (perhaps) Hitchcock into these lines, and yet the images they bring into conjunction retain a degree of inscrutability, etching themselves in the reader's mind but resisting decipherment. This effect is partly due to Follain's expert use of parataxis, placing phrases and images alongside one other in order to spark off possible correspondences or create constellations of meaning. As Jacques Réda remarks, Follain's poems typically 'set a current running between objects in juxtaposition, in the absence of any single governing metaphor'. A good example of this technique can be found in 'Signes: Signs', where a stranger lays his hand on the "thin shoulder" of a man eating in a "drab restaurant": "he thinks twice about finishing his wine/ the distant forest lies under snow". The relationship between man and stranger, restaurant interior and snowbound forest are not explained, and in the final lines of the poem the perspective shifts to that of the waitress, who has "gone pale" and thinks of "the last page/ of a not too difficult book" with its "end word" printed in "ornate capital letters". What begins as a banal, everyday scene moves decisively towards some portentous finality by its conclusion; and yet, the reader remains at a loss to say exactly what, if anything, has happened. Follain's best poetry addresses what W.S. Merwin calls "the mystery of the present", and Carson preserves and deepens that mystery in his brilliant translations.

Carson's own poems respond to the translations from Follain in a variety of ways but most often transpose images, metaphors, and ideas from rural Normandy to contemporary Belfast, as a continuation of his long-running meditation on the unsettled peace in Northern Ireland. In this regard, Follain proves to be an ideal interlocutor. For instance, in 'La guenille: The Rag', a red rag hangs from the branch of an apple tree near where "men are organizing/ in the dark times". Carson's counterpart to this poem is 'Sunset', in which "an armoured car speeds/ into the oncoming dark" along a road lined with "union/ flags" that "begin to flicker in their tatters". The echoes and correspondences set up by placing these two poems on facing pages are powerful and immediate, but the worlds that they each create are emphatically distinct. If anything, Carson's companion poems serve to draw out and set in relief the historical and political resonances that are usually more deeply buried in Follain's poems. Another example is 'The Riot', which is paired with Follain's 'Le ruine: The Ruin'. In Follain's poem, an officer dreams of reviewing his troops but is unnerved by the ruined building "with its solitary window" that borders the parade ground, a spectre of death and defeat. Carson's poem retains the image of the ruined, near-derelict building but resituates it in an urban landscape devastated by rioting:

> With sledgehammers
> they break down the walls
> of their back yards

into bricks for missiles.
A mile away
in the office block of the brick factory
every window has been bricked up
save one
by whose light the clerk
draws a line under the final reckoning
with a black metal-edged ruler.

The odd detail of the "black metal-edged ruler" is also carried over from Follain's poems, but 'The Riot' is clearly as much a translation of Carson's own poem 'Belfast Confetti' as it is a response to 'Le ruine'. Strikingly, in all three poems, the effects of violence manifest themselves in the built environment that is an arena for ordinary lives, and are also explicitly connected to acts of writing, reckoning, and making sense.

From Elsewhere is a superb collection of poems by any standards. Neither a straightforward book of translations nor simply a new collection of poems, it combines elements of both and deliberately complicates received opinions about what counts as 'original' creative work. Carson's new book, like many that preceded it, insists that creative writing is an intrinsically collaborative, dialogic practice that thrives at the borders between languages and cultural traditions, writers and their readers.

NEAL ALEXANDER

Revelling in Being Alive

Paul Durcan, *The Days of Surprise*, Harville Secker, £12
Eilean Ni Chuilleanain, *The Boys of Bluehill*, The Gallery Press, €11.95

Paul Durcan's beautiful crimson book with its dust-jacket of goldfinches takes its title from a poem in which the surprise is the election of the new Pope,

> The tide is in and Francis has come back
> From Assisi to walk again amongst us.

The poem is full of Durcan's characteristic mischief and joy, joy at the end of the reign of the 'German shepherd' and at the new dispensation of a smiling, singing pontiff. The new pope speaks for and to the humanity of the poet. This book, as all Durcan's others, is characterised by his interest in and love of life and people. The book's overarching surprise appears to be that he is here at all: that he is still living – albeit as an old man, "for is that not what I am?"; the surprise of interaction, of friendship, of late love. It is revelling in being alive, and the detail of that life and the people in it seems urgent and busy – as if it is necessary to record all, to capture life in its entire idiosyncratic colour. Because underscoring all of the joy is a counterpoint thread of death, illness and loss. It is a book of elegies for the famous – the actor David Kelly or Seamus Heaney whose, "antiphonal/Derry brogue" comes down the chimney to check that he's OK, "Are you alright down there, Poet Durcan?" – but also for ordinary people who live unnoticed and decent lives. But they are noticed – by Paul Durcan. Like Dubliner Eddie Spollen, remembered in 'Nothing Like the Funeral of a Good Man to Lift the Spirits', in which Durcan quotes the priest's eulogy,

> It was Eddie's ordinariness –
> His exceptional ordinariness – his brilliant ordinariness –
> That made him a saint – a sarcastic saint!

Durcan has his own sense of sainthood and it does not require being dead. Many of the poems have his characteristic benedictions of the names of those he loves – how wonderful to make it into a Durcan poem and be blessed in that way – and praise particularly the 'poet saints'. Brian Friel is celebrated on his 85th birthday, shared with the monk St Philip of Moscow, so that Durcan describes Friel as one who,

> spent most of his life as a married monk
> In a hermitage on Inishowen on the shores of Lough Foyle.

This poem is made all the more poignant by Friel's death since the book's publication.

Durcan's great gift is to ventriloquise, and one of the best examples here is the dramatic monologue in the irrepressible voice of Elizabeth Walsh Peavoy. This too is an elegy but in the form of one side of a visit's conversation and contains such gems as "I always read today's paper tomorrow", and "Nothing like a clean pair of knickers/ To pep up the spirits." You can just hear Durcan's wonderful voice and see his face disappear in a smile. But if Durcan can be warmly celebratory, "Hairy with euphoria", he can also use humour to condemn – he's a brilliant satirist – and his barbs are reserved for the ministers of government, for bankers and highly-paid psychiatrists and consultants whose wealth comes from the people but makes no allowance for them. In 'Meeting the Great Consultant', "the god of the hospital", he forces the man to acknowledge him before saying,

> Do you know what ? You are a perfunctory little bugger.
> But you have just done me for 600 euro – enjoy!

The book begins in childhood and poems that are hilarious but also full of the pain of his difficult relationship with his father, the judge, in 57 Dartmouth Square and comes full circle in the fantastic poem, 'Meeting a Neighbour in the GP's Waiting Room' where Durcan imagines himself a little boy again, when the man invites him in for a cup or tea and he wishes had had his marbles, his yo-yo, his conkers and his short trousers back!

Eilean Ni Chuilleanain is one of the writers Durcan blesses in *The Days of Surprise* and her Gallery collection, *The Boys of Bluehill* shares some of his collection's elegiac qualities, being also about memories and invocations of the past. But while Durcan uses a heightened, sometimes surreal, register, hers is quieter and more abstract. It is fitting that the most concrete poem is a baptism poem, one that belongs to the next generation, 'Incipit Hodie',

> When you fell into our language
> Like a fish into water,
> No wonder you were blinded by the splash you made.

In this case the child is told that, "when you reach for words they will be hard like pebbles in your hand" as if the world of the young is thus tangible and vital –contrasting with the many images in the poems of the fragility of memory, of places and time only just apprehended. In poems like 'An Information', instead of hard pebbles to be grasped, there are rooms once stood in, streets once known that can only be held momentarily and as impression. In such poems the question is used to interrogate the past but these are questions that can no longer be answered:

> (Did you sit apart? Had you washed your hands
> before entering the room? Was the water laced
> with vinegar? What did you say while it thundered?

The world seems transient, the outside flimsy, provisional, "Nothing stable except for the gleam" ('From Up Here') and inside is full of ghosts, usually unnamed, "words retreating back in the throat...":

> as in the five days she lay without a word.
> five glasses of milk huddled on a shelf.
> Congealed, the sun of a winter afternoon
> breaking through curtains, piercing the shining whey.

The questions do not make this a vague voice; Ni Chuilleanáin's voice is always strong and authoritative but you have the sense in these poems of a consciousness moving through time – the time of her own life but also of others and of history. Music is one of the vehicles of that movement, signalled in the hornpipe that gives the collection its title. Again and again there is the sense of an imperative to return,

> I might go back to the place
> where I was young...
> all I have done combines to excavate
> a channelled maze where I am escaping home. ('Youth')

The poems are poetic archaeology and often in the excavations divisions between the present and the past break down. This is true of the beautiful, 'The Skirt', based on a memory of her sister, a musician, dressed for a concert descending a stair, holding her fiddle. But as her grandfather "puts aside his graveclothes" to give a lesson in "how his mother,/his grandmother, dressed a stairway", suddenly the stairway is crowded with the traffic of the dead and, "the risers behind her/all flower in shiny blackness".

Similarly, 'Passing Palmers Green Station', which might seem to locate us in a particular place, takes her "past that other station,/where my mother lost one shoe in the gap, coming back/from the hospital where she'd left her younger daughter/among the dying". That poem ends quoting a Renaissance text, "everything lost on the earth can be found again" – a line that might have been an epigraph of this hauntingly beautiful collection.

MAUREEN BOYLE

Beautiful Rooms

Peter Sirr, *The Rooms*, The Gallery Press, €11.95
Sean O'Brien, *The Beautiful Librarians*, Picador Poetry, £9.99

In an essay on Yves Bonneyfoy's "La Maison Natale" (*Graph*, May 2013) Peter Sirr registered his general approval for the concept of "an orchestrated series of poems" and went on to develop a metaphor pertinent to the title-sequence of his latest collection: "The frame of a sequence is really a loose kind of house, a dramatic space and a series of interconnected rooms, and those connections are important. It means the different parts can speak to each other and it also means there can be an accumulation of image and mood over the duration of the series."

Sirr's poetic rooms, sonnets in the 14-line sense, or sonnets simply as short poems, are spread over three sections, 'Continual Visit', 'House Unhoused' and 'Drift'. The poems have less narrative impetus than Bonnefoy's. (Three of Bonnyfoye's poems begin with the same line, but they also move into new territory each time.) Sirr's locations are layered and impressionistic, his interiors and exteriors mirroring one another as memories of originally distinct occasions might. With their shifting reflections, they challenge linearity of time and space more intricately than Bonnefoy's poems, but are perhaps finally trapped in their aesthetic patterning. The title of the first part, 'Continual Visit' is indicative.

The collection doesn't begin with 'The Rooms'. Ten poems are placed first, independent of the sequence and each other, but in some cases thematically close to it. A very fine poem of this opening group, 'Nando's Table', describes a magical holiday-restaurant meal with friends and fauna, "all of us sitting there as if forever." The fifth sonnet in the 'Drift' section of the sequence seems to reflect, in greater tranquillity, on an identical scenario. This may be, and probably is, intentional, but it contributes to the somewhat blurry effect of much of this collection. The opening poem sets up the metaphor of the poet as map-maker, perceiving the role as bizarrely, frighteningly inclusive:

"I want to stand at the centre/ of a great clutter// mapping ashes, mapping bones..." Sirr seems to have an epic tolerance of clutter.

"Who has no house will hang his hat/ on the ramshackle, the provisional, a summer's//quick labour" he proclaims in the fourth sonnet, as if undecided between metaphorical hat-racks. Of course, the tangling accumulation is part of the strategy. The speaker may be in mourning, or some other liminal state. After death, "there's not a blade of grass that doesn't have your breath on it/ before the sun burns you back to darkness again." Even a ghost belongs to the diurnal cycle; he sleeps, wakes, visits his other old haunts, haunted by his own dead. The sense of things being simultaneously strange and familiar is formally registered in the various stanza-arrangements of the sonnets. Out of doors, death takes the shape of encroachment on the pastoral: "...a two-stroke engine/ puts manners on the hedgerow" as agribusiness comes to life before the revenant's eyes. Concrete details acquire an abstract shimmer through repetition: lake, lane, wine, oil, photos, frames, doors, hands, breath, skin, night. The night itself is, of course, only another, vaster room. There are strong hints of people – mother, father, lover – but no identities, or meetings, are simple. A favourite device is to run the narrative film backwards. Sirr mentions "the infinite/ gothics of memory" but gothics are never risked: the tone is always measured and reassuring, the hauntings somehow palliative.

The conversational rhythms of the poems to Brecht, 'Audience with BB', are bracing. This sequence is an airier showcase for Sirr's more-than-lyric ambitions. Giving poor old BB some youthful lip, his idiom is charged with the kind of energy that's missing from 'The Rooms'. "Sock it to us!/ We want the dark forests, the asphalt streets!/ Mahagonny! Chicago! Berlin!" There's a not-unpleasing Poundian echo to this mischief, with its inventive montage of translations, imitations, ripostes and challenges. Only in the 'Epilogue: Words for BB', does the sequence outlive its energy and revert to worthy word-spinning.

"They won't say: when the walnut tree shook in the wind," Brecht warned complacent contemporaries in 'In Dark Times'. "...They won't say: the times were dark /Rather: why were their poets silent?" These dicta go very much against the grain of much present thinking about poetry. We may feel that, on the contrary, the walnut tree's shaking in the wind might impart the truth about the dark times more effectively than any rant. And yet there remains a suspicion that lyric poetry enshrines the moral delusion of capitalism, privileging the individual above the collective, sacralising personal space. Sean O'Brien's poetry sometimes shares this suspicion. The tough-on-the-toffs Northern persona, fond of bashing "people like you" – nasty rich Southerners, presumably – can be irritating. But what is special and valuable about O'Brien's sensibility is that he can also write a subtly articulated personally charged poem from an outward-looking and communal sense of identity. Looking out of the train window in 'The Lost of England', his speaker observes

> Chains of ponds, canals where nothing moved, low hills
>
> I'd never walk, but knew were sacred to the childhoods
> of the unknown and invisible who seemed to wait
> there in the wings of that unceasing afternoon
> as though our going were a signal to resume their secret lives.

These lines make generous space for an imagination other than the speaker's.

O'Brien's technique can be allusive and glancing: he shares some Francophile tendencies with Peter Sirr (see 'Wedding Breakfast' and the beautiful 'Café de l'Imprimerie'). But predominantly he belongs to that significant two-generation group of politically radical British poets born between the 1930s and '50s, give or take a few years: it includes Alan Brownjohn and Douglas Dunn, to mention two who are named in these pages. Their radicalism often finds expression via the sense of place. In honouring the numinous, they reconcile the haughty management (the Muse) and the impatient work-force (the ideals of social justice).

CAROL RUMENS

The Playful and the Inherently Sad

Don Paterson, *40 Sonnets*, Faber, £14.99
Christopher Reid, *The Curiosities*, Faber, £14.99

In *40 Sonnets*, Don Paterson not only explores the density and structure of the traditional sonnet form but also experiments with it in order to illustrate its flexibility. Thematically what is most striking about this volume is how mystical some of the insights are, how much they depend on the experience and explanation of those moments from which little can be deduced but which are powerful indicators of spiritual claims on us. One of the best examples of this is the holy sonnet 'Lacrima', a poem that leaves the name of Jesus Christ unsaid, as if only the divine terms of the incarnation and the tears of the crucifixion remain. The poem begins in disbelief and anger, then moves through forgiveness toward illumination. The second stanza is a telling example of how Paterson can make such moments of struggle and illumination contemporary, living expressions of the invisible made visible:

> One drop belled at the fracture in his side,
> and then a stream, a flood, a tidal race –
> all he was was one huge tear. In his place
> there stood a human shape cut from the void,
> an empty tearless glory. I walked in
> and now I wear it like a second skin.

The following poem in the volume, 'Francesca Woodman', considers the American photographer who committed suicide in her early twenties (which is relevant in a poem about ghosts), and whose female nudes can be challenging black and white portraits (this aspect is reiterated even more strongly in the later poem 'On Woodman's Photography'). Some of her photographs, however, are blurred images that seem on the verge of disappearing, as though trying to hide from the viewer. Paterson aptly describes this effect: "We don't exist – We only dream we're here– / This means we never die – We disappear". He also catches the sense of vulnerability in some of the photographs and how the spectral quality is as much a reflection of our estrangement as it is a spiritual value: "All rooms will hide you, if you stand just so. / All ghosts know this. That's really all they know." 'Two', 'A Vow', and 'A Threshold' take some of the same issues of the ineffability, fear of loss and almost vanishing sense of being into the realm of personal relationships.

Among its many themes, these subtle and beautiful poems articulate themes of love and distance ('Here', 'The Six'). 'Here' is the opening sonnet and has to be quoted in full to grasp its intricacy (the beating heart recalls the mother, the mother the sea and all these the sense in this life of being shipwrecked far from home):

> I must quit sleeping in the afternoon.
> I do it for my heart, but all too soon
> my heart has called it off. It does not love me.
> If it downed tools, there'd soon be nothing of me.
> Its hammer-beat says you are, not I am.
> It prints me off here like a telegram.
> What do I say? How can the lonely word
> know who has sent it out, or who had heard?
> Long years since I came round in her womb
> enough myself to know I was not home,
> my dear sea up in arms at the wrong shore
> and her loud heart like a landlord at the door.
> Where are we know? What misdemeanor sealed
> my transfer? Mother, why so far afield?

'Wave' considers how the imagined other calls forth the deepest aspects of the inner life, while 'The Air' meditates on the origin of metaphysics ("When will the air stop breathing? Will it all/ come to nothing, if nothing came to this?"). 'The Self-Illuminated' examines the mystical life of a martyr and how literature can temper suffering. 'Funeral Prayer' is a poignant elegy that in its depth, cadence, and simplicity recalls some of Yeats's best elegies:

> He has left time. Perhaps we feel
> we are the ghosts and him the real –
> so fixed and constant does he seem,

so starlike.
[...]yet of all the words
we know, his name was the most dear.
We give thanks he was spoken here.

Paterson, like Muldoon, puts the sonnets to different uses: there is a fourteen-word sonnet in Scots, 'At the Perty'. There are stirring political poems ('The Foot'); others are savage denunciations ('The Big Listener') or comical takes ('To Dundee City Council'). There are poems of social satire ('An Incarnation') and literary satire ('Requests', 'A Scholar'). The most experimental and playful poem is 'Séance', which begins with the phonetic rendering "Speke" and then distorts the work into "see" and "spiikess" among a number of other combinations. It is as though the spirit world, by speaking in riddles, ultimately reduces language to its parts. There is also a eponymous sonnet on the television show, 'House'. Finally, there is a prose poem, as well as a traditional sonnet, on writing: 'The Version' and 'The Fable of the Open Book' respectively. All are written with the same adeptness, assured in both theme and craft. But it is the poems of fleeting experience like 'Nostalgia', the conflict of soul and body in 'A Calling' and 'Souls' and those poems about seduction and love ('Sentinel' and 'Mercies') that probe most deeply, and so leave the reader feeling the same undefinable sense of having grasped something profound. Paterson fittingly ends the last sonnet of the sequence with an observation that underlies many of the strengths of the volume: "we lay and looked up at a sky so clear / there was nothing in the world to prove our turning / but our light heads, and the wind's lung". There is something almost pre-Socratic in defining our understanding through the elements. Then again, it may simply be the role of poet to make the abstract concrete.

Early in his career Christopher Reid was identified with the Martian poets. Though some critical opinion has it that he has moved away from that initial influence, he has certainly retained his playfulness and defamiliarization, which are exhibited in many of the poems in *The Curiosities*, but perhaps nowhere more than in the concept of the volume itself: over seventy poems fixated on the letter C. To emphasize the centrality of the joke (and the inherent sadness), the volume begins with 'The Clowns', which with the opening question, "Who is whose clown, precisely? The answer, "His Majesty El Rey de Jamón", tells us that Reid, much like Wallace Stevens, is a "witty bufón". But all is not wit in this collection (though much is). 'The Cry' is an unsettling unfolding of the uncanniness that is announced in the first line: "The child woke to a cry not his." The poem moves through the various reasons for the cry, typical ones for a child, and then ends with the fascination children (and adults) have for what disturbs them:

> But the rest of the cry
> had put up a fight against itself:
> an urgent, delirious skirmish.
> Which it must win. Which it did,
> with a short-lasting whimper
> of triumph and release.
> In the peace that followed,
> the child lay awake, unable to explain
> why he was stirred by a thing
> so ugly, so sad and so frightening;
> nor why he wanted to hear it again.

The following poem, 'The Coin' gives a clever turn to the serious subject of crossing the river with Charon, boatman of the underworld. It is told from the boatman's point of view. 'The Calabash' takes the very rounded female shape of this gourd as a premise for the creation of woman by God, and the conversation with Man about it. Man is sceptical of the difference between "the pure shape / that had first caught his fancy; both virginal and gravid, / suspended improbably from that scruffy tree", and the "lovely roundness" that God had created with such care. Woman also "had her proliferating doubts". 'The Call' reiterates some of these themes as they arise in the animal world.

Reid's perspective as a poet in such poems is well explained in lines from 'The Children':

> His stubby arms stick out
> stiff as a crucifixion;

his lower body's as slack
as a deposition from the cross;
from his new, calmly enjoyed
eminence he can survey
both the world of sorrow and loss
and his sister's beautiful hair.

He views sensuality and suffering from an ironical aesthetic distance. Other moods and themes in the volume are tenderness ('The Colt'); gender bending ('The Costume'); lasciviousness ('The Chill' and more subtly 'The Café'); ecstasy and art ('The Chisel'); the erotics of art ('The Catapult', 'The Critics', 'The Couch'); sensuality ('The Cherry', 'The Collarbone') and its potential and vivid violence ('The Cougar', 'The Caterwaul'); fear of sexuality ('The Celibate', 'The Coward') and the refuge of sexuality ('The Courtesies'). 'The Corbel' unveils the profane nature of the sacred, while 'The Cottage', in a play on Yeats and Augustine, considers the potential purity of sexuality despite the link between excrement and sex. There is a beautiful poem after Rilke ('The Courtesan') that captures the feminine personification of La Serenissima in the last decadence of the Venetian empire. Then there is the transgressive, pedophilic 'The Craving', written without comment or objection. Though I am not sure the overly indifferent 'The Craving' qualifies, Reid's distant, humorous perspective provides him with insight into brutality that a more openly sympathetic and emotive view might not have (at the least this methods suits the poet). The memory of corporal punishment in 'The Canes', like 'The Crowbar', is a perfect example of this. The junior masters suddenly had a craze for canes that turned into "police-state caprice and brute force". The "odd thing" was that they "christened their weapons / with old-fashioned girls' names". The whimsical nature of this sadistic and strangely erotic practice is thereby conveyed with a light touch that makes the brutal crack of the punishment felt more keenly by the reader. 'The Cacophony', on the other hand, reverses the roles so that it is the students who are tormenting the teacher.

There are also philosophical and psychoanalytic poems like 'The Calm', 'The Crossroads', and 'The Cyborgs', which bring a different dimension and illustrate the full repertoire of the poet. The last of which imagines the robotic beings as the troubadours of their times. It is an interesting take on what technique (computers versus double sestinas) actually means and how they have and will always intersect. Similarly, 'The Cowhand' and 'The Conceit' are written in western American parlance and archaic English respectively, and show how much of a master Reid is of his language. 'The Courier', a modern take on a bawdy fourteenth-century Welsh poet's work, displays a similar sense of craft. 'The Caryatids' begins with the erotic basis of art and ends with a contemplation of death and our separateness as we each bear the load of mortality:

> I fear the equal spaces between us mean
> that, while we share our load equally,
> we're trapped by it, too; feet on plinths,
> head jammed against ceilings, we're
> the precise size, the very measure,
> of our own imprisonment and servitude,
> and can never aspire to any gesture
> of non-compliance. So our defiance
> must work more subtly. Aided by time,
> by the weather, by our steadfast wills,
> we crumble as we stand. Our suffering
> is sublime, a slow stone death,
> and we take pride in enduring it together.

'The Capsule' and 'The Chaos' describe similar scenarios of our sometimes uneasily shared and distinctly lonely destinies. This weight is appreciated in a volume that is once in a while too jokey and light (for example, the last poem 'The Centaurs'). 'The Curse' (after Catullus), on the other hand, is casually but deeply resonant. As Ruskin observed, sometimes an artist's flaw is his or her strength and that is certainly the case with Christopher Reid. His humor and light touch often plumb the deeps if one is attentive to his descriptions of the fall.

JEFFERSON HOLDRIDGE

Striking Sparks from Stone Repeatedly

Caitriona O'Reilly, *Geis*, Bloodaxe, £9.99
Rachael Boast, *Pilgrim's Flower*, Picador, £9.99

After a gap of nine years since her critically-acclaimed second collection, *The Sea Cabinet*, Caitríona O'Reilly's eagerly-anticipated third collection *Geis* (pronounced 'geysh') is worth every second of the wait. The book fully bears witness to the weight of those years. In Irish mythology a 'geis' is a supernatural taboo or an injunction on behaviour, similar to being under a spell. It is both a curse and a gift. As O'Reilly explains in an interview with Wake Forest University Press, the geis "had a psychological significance for me . . . related to blocks or compulsions in the personality, our self-limiting behaviours. This is the sense in which it is used in the title sequence of the book, which describes a time of personal trauma and the fallout from that."

The 'fledgling notes' of the collection's opening poem, 'Ovum', both hint at the nature of that trauma and signal the poet's keen interest in "the meat / of the word", per se. With its precise selection of 'o-words' and the order in which the poet chooses to present them – "from oblation and obloquy to oxlip and ozone" – the poem suggests how the collection will move: from considering something offered up to God, perhaps, through an examination of self-censure and reproach, to emerge ultimately in the flowering of the natural world albeit tempered by mankind's effects on that world. Though not divided into sections, this is a book of two halves. The first half comprises intensely personal, inward-looking lyrics mostly written in single unbroken stanzas or in unrhymed couplets and tercets; the second half turns to look outwards and consider the wider world, with the poems often expanding in both form and scope, including a number in blockier or longer-lined stanzas, and even a ghazal. The pivot between the two halves is the word 'snowdrop' at the end of 'The Winter Suicides'; it is no accident that the title sequence of eight poems, which broke the poet's spell of five years of not writing, is placed immediately before it.

Geis contains rich imagery throughout, some of which is familiar from O'Reilly's earlier collections: sea, whales, birds, light. In particular, there are both close and distant echoes of all six end-words ("room", "roof", "skin", "glass", "dinner", "bone") from her excellent sestina 'Thin', a first person account of anorexia, in her début collection *The Nowhere Birds*. Three other images seem especially dynamic in *Geis*: thread, stone, and leaf (or tree). Thread is both obsession and compulsion, "that old snarl in the brain again that will not unfurl" ('Riddle'). The speaker of 'Ariadne' reflects how:

> It will take me a lifetime
> to unpick this,
>
> finding the right thread
> to pull and unravel,
> pull and unravel.

Indeed, the book itself is a little like this. There is a lot of depth here, a lot to be discovered; it will reward many re-readings. Stone, too, can represent the block of obsession, but is more complex than thread. It occurs in many guises – as egg, pill, pendulum, atom, amber, sun – sometimes writhing, sometimes radiant. From the second-half poem, 'Clotho', an ekphrastic response to a nineteenth-century sculpture by Camille Claudel depicting an old woman ensnared in her very long hair, it is clear from both thread and stone imagery just how far the speaker has come:

> And in the end it was easiest to let go
> of all that vigilance, the endless distaff-to-spindle rigour
> of your compulsions, and allow the silks to snarl.
> . . .
> . . .
> You had never believed that life was what happened to us.
> Rather it was to strike sparks from stone repeatedly,
> Acts of creation, clearly, are happening once more.

Of the worldly poems in the second half of the collection, a number are truly magnificent: 'Polar' (in which a polar bear becomes the spirit of the arctic); 'Blue Poles' (an extraordinary ekphrastic elegy for Jackson Pollock, with reference to the not-really-round-the-world yachtsman Donald Crowhurst); 'The Antikythera Mechanism' (a long-lined poem concerning an ancient computer designed to predict the movement of heavenly bodies in which "The yes-no, no-yes of the pendulum" becomes a metaphor for existential questioning); and 'The Airship Era'. This latter poem's shoal of four eight-line stanzas swimming like zeppelins high above the landscape "of that epauletted century" might stand for the collection as a whole, and the paradox of the geis at its centre: "how lighter than air they were. / They did not understand, as they fell continually upwards, / how the nature of the element was the price of their rising". As Milan Kundera asserts near the beginning of *The Unbearable Lightness of Being*, "The only certainty is: the lightness/weight opposition is the most mysterious, most ambiguous of all". The lightness of touch of O'Reilly's poetry and the weight of its impact are born not of self-negation, but by bravely and honestly wrestling with her blocks and compulsions through her expert use of the medium of words.

As the book nears its end, the weight of stone diminishes and the green imagery is allowed to unfurl. In 'Triptych', an at times Larkinesque meditation on three aspects of Lincoln Cathedral, stone is "soft" and "blond" and used to build "stone trunks that soar to the clerestory". Elsewhere, the mood is leavened by occasional flashes of wry humour: "Who in their bleakest hour has not considered Iowa?" By the final poem, 'Komorebi' (an untranslatable Japanese word used to describe the effect of sunlight filtering through the branches and leaves of trees), stone has disappeared entirely, or perhaps has transmuted into "sun", and we are left instead with an image of light "in radiant bands ascending the birch trunks", and a cormorant "dazzled to absolute / by the word and the world's beauty." We are dazzled too, elated almost, by the speaker's – the poet's – ultimate achievement of transcendence.

Rachael Boast's second collection, *Pilgrim's Flower*, is not what it might seem from a glance at its cover: twee lyrics about churches and flowers and walking. Whilst all these elements are here, they are put to the service of a much bigger project. This is a fiercely intelligent exploration of self-image and gender identity. It should be read as a companion to Boast's award-winning début collection, Sidereal, the themes and structure of which it both mirrors and develops. Indeed, one sequence, 'Other Roads', begun in the first collection, is continued here. The books are twins. The layout of the poems in each collection alerts us to this: Sidereal is divided into two roughly equal halves (of 33 and 36 pages of poems, respectively) numbered simply 'I' and 'II'; so – precisely – is *Pilgrim's Flower*. This double doubling, this mirrored mirroring, becomes the poet's central conceit.

Pilgrim's Flower opens with a poem in two sentences of extended syntax, 'The Place of Five Secrets', an ekphrastic response to Jean Cocteau's film Beauty and the Beast. From its first line, "Resembling Cocteau, the two statues in the pillars", the poem sets out the book's chief thematic concerns of self-image and gender identity – and also its interest in love – through the interplay of Bête "who is not himself, even on a good day", and Belle, who with "her love's second sight revives him as he is, / and not as other see him". These themes are developed in the next six poems (sonnets and poems in quatrains) which are presented in pairs, the form of each exactly reflecting the form of the poem on the facing page. Here "the border / . . . isn't all that clear"; things are "half-said"; there are diversions and disguises. These poems also introduce us to the other important elements that will be encountered on our journey through the collection: homage to various literary figures, sometimes involving translations or versions of their work (here Akhmatova and Thomas Chatterton, later Coleridge, Sappho, Machado, Shakespeare, and Cocteau again); pilgrimages to cathedrals and churches, especially in Bristol and Scotland and the north of England; and the perennial question of time. Note the fluid identity of many of the literary figures Boast chooses to pay homage to, and the concept of "homage" itself, with its etymological root in "homo" – man. All this material is very cleverly handled, including in the longer sequences, adding great depth to a collection which invites many re-readings. If ever there is a danger of it all becoming too highly intellectualized, Boast often brings the tone back down with a colloquial word or phrase – the "posh" peacock in 'Song of', for example.

Boast possesses superb formal skills. In particular, she is a master of the turn. In the twin sonnets 'Reciprocity' and 'Double Life', form works absolutely in tandem with content as each poem of two seven-line stanzas turns precisely at its mid-point. Her turns are often indicated simply by "And" or "But", conjunctions which act as signposts to help us follow the path of her thoughts, and sometimes of her walks too. In the pilgrimage poem, 'Balmerino Abbey', there are at least six turns before we watch the poem, like the murmuration of starlings in its final image:

> ... lifting off again and inclining
> into that vanishing point of airborne forms
> un-blackening at the narrowest angle
> of themselves [...]

Elsewhere, there are briefer moments of imagery, deftly drawn: "The sun's afloat, / jubilant as a smashed champagne glass / left over from a wedding party"; "boats in their moorings – / ... lined up / like notes in a glockenspiel".

The collection finishes with 'Desperate Meetings of Hermaphrodites', another excellent ekphrastic response to a Cocteau film which, "seeing as the mirror / is a poem", mirrors the opening poem. In this final poem, however, Boast extends her syntax with controlled fluidity across its entire length in a single sentence, to end by "finding the dripping statue, from whose mouth / all this had come, is dressing up as you." In case we were still in any doubt about the over-arching project of the book, the 'General note' at the end of the Notes winks at us – coquettishly – twice: Repeated references to the name "Thomas", seven in total, were not intentional on behalf of the author but can nevertheless be taken as referring to Didymus, "The Twin". In Aramaic "Thomas" also means "twin".' And we are sent scurrying back to the start of this wonderful collection to track down the seven Thomases and marvel once again at Boast's brilliant, mature, exploration of "guises revealed not as forgeries / but the mutable self fluttering by candlelight."

EMMA MUST

Paradise Restored

Mark Doty, *Deep Lane*, Jonathan Cape, 2015, £10

Mark Doty's *Deep Lane* is a collection of highs and lows. Whether literally high "on the top level/of the George Washington Bridge" ('Immanence'), or low "down on my knees" in the opening line of the first incarnation of 'Deep Lane' (there are nine poems that share this title in this his ninth collection); whether illegally high courtesy of "the syringe/with the shattered stuff of possibility" ('Crystal'), or figuratively plunged into an underworld in an outpatient clinic where one man's footwear "catches my breath/with the name printed across/ the tongues of his shoes://OSIRIS, in bold letters" ('Underworld'): Doty intentionally leads us on a tour of this world's heavens and hells and longed-for lands, as Wallace Stevens identified them in his 'An Ordinary Evening in New Haven' back in 1950. Stevens, an obvious precursor for, and clear influence on, Doty, revelled in making the very ordinariness of America the subject of sublime poetic departures from that reality both to emphasise its incontrovertible and essential realness and to reinforce its centrality in the making of poetry. This is the line, one that is part of a particularly American poetic tradition, that Doty has followed, explored and now, with this collection, extended in poems whose beauty is that of "heave and contorted thrust[s]" ('Amagansett Cherry').

Deep Lane is not a collection for the faint-hearted. Whatever Doty's considerable talents as a poet – and they are considerable – this, like previous Doty works, is a collection of hard living, of losses, but is also one of endurance. It seeks for that which it writes: the redemptive power of art in the face of relentless mortality. *Deep Lane* is all about the oppositions that define this world; or, if not oppositions, the pairings that characterise so much of what we call life. Life and death, and their interminable ups and downs, figure prominently, as do cemeteries, memories of family and friends lost either to time, illness or suicide. The first five poems are all titled 'Deep Lane' and the repetition serves to disorient as much as it maps our way through the work that lies ahead. Doty brings us into the collection at ground level

in a poem that spans out to encompass references to the late Seamus
Heaney ("all day we go digging,//harrowing, rooting deep. Spade-
plunge/and trowel"), to Elizabeth Bishop (the "sweet turned-down
gas flame" here revisits the waters of Bishop's 'The Bight' that are "the
color of the gas flame turned down as low as possible"), and finally to
Deborah Digges (her married name perhaps the unfortunate, though
here buried, initiator of this poem), an award-winning poet and
friend of Doty's who apparently took her own life in 2009. The second
'Deep Lane' poem lightens the load a little, Doty resetting the balance
toward black humour as his dog Ned uproots one of four poles placed
to mark out a new grave in a nearby cemetery. And so *Deep Lane* is set
on its way, moving as it will between the poles of loss and abandon in a
collection that insists upon writing the "Beauty that does not disguise
the wound" ('Ars Poetica: 14th Street Gym').

Doty excels in such an exercise. Indeed, he hasn't been better at it
than he is here. All of the themes and flourishes, the signature moves
and the poetic high tones of his earlier volumes are on display in *Deep
Lane*. But there is something more as well. The poems are not abstract
digressions on the production of art – though 'To Jackson Pollock' is a
glorious refutation of what indeed has just been claimed, Doty's paean
to Pollock's "huge canvases" as "prayers" its own masterstroke within
this collection – they are rooted, have purchase, and continually
exhibit "torque and fervor" ('Amagansett Cherry'). His willingness to
peel back the outer layers of meaning in language, to allow immanent
meanings to resurface across poems – and collections – fits him firmly
in an American tradition of poetry that traces notable predecessors
in Elizabeth Bishop as well as Stevens. Poetry, for Doty, performs a
similar task, indeed the endless task, as mapped out and laid down by
both Stevens and Bishop. "Poetry is a response to the daily necessity
of getting the world right" as Stevens (for once) simplified it in his
Opus Posthumous; for Bishop "life and the memory of it" become "so
compressed/they've turned into each other" ('Poem'). Doty has taken
heed of such words, and the evidence is everywhere on show in how he
deploys his own words throughout *Deep Lane*.

We pay attention to his own attentiveness to all of the words under
his control. His finding of the right ones to describe the things of this

world has long been a central motif of his work: return to 'Description' or 'A Display of Mackerel' in his 1995 collection Atlantis for evidence of this twenty-one years ago. "It's what I do, the nature of my attention, the signature of my selfhood: finding the words", as he explains in The Art of Description (2010). The impulse is a repetitive need "[t]o refuse silence" and "[t]o arrive at exactitude in order to experience the satisfaction of matching words to the world" (The Art of Description). While some may characterise Doty's verbal eloquence and dexterity, his sifting through language for exactly the right language, to be more academic than 'real' (whatever that might be), they are missing one of several points. Doty's unpicking of language is the latest version of American poetry about its own work: it is Frost seeking the gold in the ore; it is Whitman (the subject of 'What is the Grass?' here and its own return to a humourously annotated Leaves of Grass) pronouncing a democratic American poetic; it is Emerson (one of two epigraphs to *Deep Lane*; the other is Mark Twain) calling for a poetry fit for and true to American contexts.

Deep Lane may have missed out on the 2015 T.S. Eliot Prize – though Doty had already claimed the honour of being the first American to claim that particular award, for his 1993 collection *My Alexandria* – but it is nevertheless a volume that merits more than simply passing acclaim. *Deep Lane* marks Doty's pre-eminence in American poetry in the first decades of the twenty-first century. Here he leads us through graveyards and side streets and underworlds and Eden; we pass through nine circuits of 'Deep Lane', pay homage to the 'King of Fire Island' (itself an hommage to Bishop's 'The Moose'? – the following poem in Doty's volume is titled 'Little Mammoth' after all, recalling Bishop's erroneously titled 'The Man-Moth'?). We pitch between death and beauty; are exposed to the four elements of earth, wind, fire and water; encounter paradises lost (and yes, Milton merits a mention, in 'Underworld', right in the centre of the collection) and paradises regained; and finally emerge from *Deep Lane* "descending from a ferocious intention" ('Amagansett Cherry'), tumultuous, yet in equilibrium.

PHILIP MCGOWAN

Thanks for Sharing: Post-Internet Poetry?

Sam Riviere, *Kim Kardashian's Marriage*, Faber, £10.99
Frances Leviston, *Disinformation*, Picador £9.99

2015: the year of car hacks, the "quantified self" intensified by health apps and Fitbits, and of ever leaking cloud data; the year that exposed Amazon's extensive metric and data-driven analysis not only of its customers but its employees, and Google restructured its company so it could spend more time attempting to bring the internet to remote areas via helium balloons. Two collections from 2015 take on this information age and pose questions about how poetry might respond to or challenge it.

Sam Riviere's *Kim Kardashian's Marriage* wears its post-internet status proudly on its sleeve. Like the poet's first collection, *81 Austerities*, the poems here were published first as a blog, and loudly signal the language of the web: 'Thanks for Sharing' concludes the five-line 'the new sunsets', with its appropriately bland celebration of "Sunset thru the trees". More urgently – though often not really discussed in in some reviews of the book – the poems of Riviere's second collection are made *out of* the web. The book was written by Googling the title of each poem and rearranging the results, in a technique of that belongs (at least as far as certain internet commentators are concerned) in the 'Flarf' tradition. The 72 poems here echo the 72 days of Kim Kardashian's first marriage not in any direct reflection on the selfie-obsessed entrepreneur/master manipulator of viral celebrity; instead according to the algorithm by which Riviere has combined two sets of nine words in eight different ways (borrowing terms from Kardashian's make-up regime as section headings), 72 is the inevitable number of two-word titles he produces. Less clear is how Riviere has decided on the title words themselves. One of these being "hardcore", however, the reconstituted text is clearly harvested from pages concerning the internet's most unique and enduring products. These are not only the new brand of celebrity created by "hardcore" file-sharing fans, but hardcore pornography:

if it were all wrapped up in a box and sent to you
that box would read ....
Beautiful Pornstar Cleopatra Hardcore Orgy
('beautiful hardcore')

Tellingly, another of Riviere's title words is "sincerity". It is, of course, the rejection of sincerity or authenticity which accounts for there being few conventional or stand-alone poems here. 'The new heaven', in which the heavily repeated lines become a mock-religious refrain (before directing us to "...The New Heaven & The New Earth's official profile,/ including the latest music albums, songs, music videos and more updates") is notable both for its length and for the sense that it crafts a response to the webstream in ways other than adopting its language. Elsewhere within *Kim Kardashian's Marriage*, only occasionally does an "I" emerge which might be mistaken as biographical. And, of course, this is the point. Appropriating the inarticulate and fragmented language of the web, the poems conceptually make an atomised wifi-dependent consciousness part of their very investigation. "How much remixes can you make" asks "infinity hardcore"; "I DO NOT OWN OR TAKE CREDIT/ FOR THIS SONG" reads a line in 'american dust', underscoring the shared and impersonal methods of composition at work here. In this way – Googled, borrowed, cut-and-paste – the poems echo the web's multi-authored randomness, its eternally reconfigurable nature, endlessly passing from one subject to the next. "After the internet", this work and its fans proclaim, "poetry can never be the same".

Yet another definition of internet or post-internet poetry might be poetry which shares the conditions created by the internet. That is to say, poetry which is – like Kim Kardashian's first marriage – if not bullshit exactly, then virtual rather than "real": poetry which is mechanical in its techniques, self-advertising as a substitute for the sustained and silent slog (in the manner of some Twitter activity), and designed for immediate, though perhaps not lasting, appreciation by "like"-minded fans. *Kim Kardashian's Marriage* clearly has its swiping, smartphone finger firmly on the cultural pulse, but by point of contrast it was something of a shock in the late 1990s to discover that Medbh McGuckian's poetry was largely composed of assembled fragments of borrowed text. No such scandal has followed Riviere's provocations. McGuckian's postmodern antics (like Paul Muldoon's) posed a challenge to a literary culture still invested, to some extent, in ideas authorial authenticity and coherence – while also anticipating the conditions of hypertext in a frankly weird way. These conditions having arrived, it is less clear whether *Kim Kardashian's Marriage* marks a critique of contemporary tastes or merely a reflection of them.

Disinformation, Frances Leviston's second collection, also concerns itself with pervasive discourses which cloud what might be understood as "reality", and how both identity and poetry may be complicit with "false data". A recurrent motif here is the notion of untruth, revealed at what looked set to be a point of disclosure. In the title poem, a woman preparing for a birthday party "suddenly glimpses the screen of false data behind which she lives". It concludes:

> Out the kitchen window
> the whirligig turns, metal spokes
> merciless as diagrams
> cutting the air
> no clothing softens, tiny gems
> icing the nodes where their lines intersect.
> every extant leaf is fixed
> with glitter where the glue's dried clear.

The confusion here between the natural and the constructed, with its near-invisible glaze of glue, is picked up throughout several keenly-observed object poems in the book's first section. In 'A Token', a cocktail umbrella is "a finch in the Dolomites/ glued to a tree". 'IUD', with its self-explanatory interest in the artificial regulation of reproduction, gives way to 'Iresine', a flowering plant which appears both artificial ("shocking pink and plasticky-looking") and oddly sexual (a "flinching clitoral architecture". Google Images confirms that this is accurate). Best of all, 'Parma Violet' celebrates, apparently effortlessly but within a tightly controlled alternate rhyme scheme, an old portrait "supposed" to be of a distant cousin or great grandmother. In fact it is revealed as "a junk-shop likeness of a stranger", whose invented identity and history makes her, in turn, no less kin.

In these poems, up-close prosaic description ('cylinders of sausage', 'yellow cheese') gives way to disorientating effects. 'The Bridge in the Mirror' gets us somehow from a bathtub to political protesters, and a "mini-bar committee" described as both "draft dodgers" and "working class heroes". In 'Trimmings: Periptero', image piles on image so rapidly and elliptically as to approach free-association: "Apparently/peripatetic, it pops up/wherever I go, glistening/on my shoulder: gold epaulette,/abatross...". There is a slightly self-conscious seriousness at work here and its message is *we do not know what we think we know*. Disorientation too might be the theme of 'GPS' – which is, of course, not about a GPS but a snow globe. This image of the sealed world, under its "smooth glass dome", is picked up in 'Paperweight' ("the earth's atmosphere in miniature") and is suggestive, again, of the way in which *Disinformation* perceives distorting cultural forces seamlessly encircling us all. The political and economic dimensions of this false consciousness are not far away. 'Pyramid', in which a saleswoman touts "a lifestyle just like mine", sees construction work halted and the (housing) bubble burst in its witty final lines:

> Through the cranes'
> necks the cloud-burst rings,
> across the clad-
> stone hotel still missing
>
> its penthouse, it punchline,
> bucketing down
> like the old cartoon
> where a skeleton drinks champagne.

Yet if Leviston often looks so hard at things that they go out of focus, poems from the book's final section confirm that it is, nevertheless, worth looking. Here note-booky poems such as 'The Taiga', 'Caribou' and 'Kassandra' scrupulously observe and document their environments and experiences. The obvious debt to Elizabeth Bishop (as well as, elsewhere, to the syllabics of Marianne Moore) is another a welcome sign *Disinformation*'s ambition – and also suggests an alternative approach to that of Sam Riviere in the difficult terrain of contemporary poetry. In a world where the distinction between reality and virtual reality has grown bewilderingly tenuous, it suggests an impulse to look beyond the bubbles of disinformation with which literature too may be complicit – a tech-enhanced obsession with the new and awesome, not to mention standards of evaluation driven by metrics – to the irreplaceably human in poetry. That is, for language which accurate, deep-rooted and slowly-grown: less 'sunlight thru trees', perhaps, than actual sunset through actual trees.

LEONTIA FLYNN

NEAL ALEXANDER lectures in English literature at Aberystwyth University. He is the author of *Ciaran Carson: Space, Place, Writing* (2010); co-editor of *Poetry & Geography* (2013) and *Regional Modernisms* (2013); and an editor of the peer-reviewed journals, *Literary Geographies* and *The International Journal of Welsh Writing in English*.

ELIZABETH BARRETT has published four collections of poetry, most recently *A Dart of Green and Blue* (Arc, 2010). She lives in Sheffield, England, where she works as a University Lecturer in Education.

FAYE BOLAND has had poems published in *Literature Today, The Shop, Revival, Crannóg, Orbis, Wordlegs, Ropes, Headstuff, Silver Apples, The Blue Max Review* and *Speaking for Sceine Chapbooks, Vols I and II*. In 2014 her poetry was included in *Visions: An Anthology of Emerging Kerry Writers*. Her poem 'Silver Bracelet' was shortlisted in 2013 for the Poetry on the Lake XIII International Poetry Competition.

MAUREEN BOYLE lives in Belfast. She was runner-up in the Patrick Kavanagh Poetry Prize in 2004 and Highly Commended in 2015. In 2007 she was awarded the Ireland Chair of Poetry Prize and the Strokestown International Poetry Prize. She was the recipient of an Artist's Career Enhancement Award from the Arts Council of Northern Ireland in 2011. In 2013 she won the Fish Short Memoir Prize, was shortlisted for the Fish Poetry Prize and was a finalist in the Mslexia single poem competition. Her poems have been published in *The Honest Ulsterman, From the Fishhouse, Fortnight, The Yellow Nib, Poetry Ireland Review, Mslexia, Incertus*.

RUTH CARR lives in Belfast, where she works as a freelance tutor. In 1985 she edited *The Female Line* (under the name Hooley). She co-edited *The Honest Ulsterman* and she is a member of the Word of Mouth collective. Her two collections of poems are *There Is a House* and *The Airing Cupboard*, both published by Summer Palace Press.

ENDA COYLE GREENE's first collection, *Snow Negatives*, won the Patrick Kavanagh Award in 2006 and was published by the Dedalus Press the following year. Her second collection, *Map of the Last*, also from the Dedalus Press, was published in 2013. She holds an MA (Dist.) in English, Creative Writing, from the Seamus Heaney Centre for Poetry at Queens's University, Belfast.

OWEN GALLAGHER is from Glasgow, and lives in London. His poems have been published widely in the UK, Ireland and abroad. He has awards from The London Arts Board and The Society of Authors. His most recent book *A Good Enough Love*, 2015, Salmon Poetry, Ireland, www.salmonpoetry was nominated for the T.S. Eliot Prize in 2015.

ELAINE GASTON is from Ireland's north coast. Her first collection, *The Lie of the Land*, was published last year. In 2015 she also received a Commendation in the Vincent Buckley Poetry Prize and she was long-listed for the Oxford Brookes International Poetry Competition. She currently lectures at Ulster University.

JEFF HOLDRIDGE is Professor of English at Wake Forest University and Director of Wake Forest University Press. His critical study *The Poetry of Paul Muldoon* appeared in 2008 from The Liffey Press.

Born in 1975 in County Tyrone, **NICK LAIRD** is a poet, novelist and screenwriter. He lives in New York. His last collection *Go Giants* was published in 2013. A new collection, *Glitch*, is forthcoming.

HANNAH LOWE's memoir *Long Time, No See* is published by Periscope. Her new collection, Chan is due from Bloodaxe in June. She lives in London and teaches at Kingston University.

PETER MCDONALD's *Collected Poems* appeared in 2012. In 2016, he publishes two new volumes of poetry: *Herne the Hunter* (Carcanet) and *The Homeric Hymns* (Carcanet/Fyfield).

ERIKA MEITNER is the author of four books of poems, including *Copia* (BOA Editions, 2014), and *Ideal Cities* (Harper Perennial, 2010), which was a 2009 National Poetry Series winner. Her poems have appeared in *Best American Poetry 2011*, *Tin House*, *The New Republic*, *Virginia Quarterly Review*, *The Kenyon Review*, and elsewhere. In 2015 she was the US-UK Fulbright Scholar in Creative Writing at the Seamus Heaney Centre for Poetry at Queen's University Belfast. She is currently an associate professor of English at

Virginia Tech, where she directs the MFA Program in Creative Writing.

OLIVER MORT is from Belfast, Northern Ireland. His poems have appeared in various magazines and journals over the years.

EMMA MUST is studying part-time for a PhD in the Seamus Heaney Centre, focusing on eco-poetry and eco-criticism. Her debut poetry pamphlet, *Notes on the Use of the Austrian Scythe*, was published by Templar in 2015.

KEVIN QUINN has previously published poems in *Fortnight* and *Poetry Ireland Review*. His talks on poets and poetry include as subjects W B Yeats, Seamus Heaney, Robert Frost and Poems for Christmas.

JOHN REDMOND is a Reader in Creative Writing at the University of Liverpool. His third book of poems, *The Alexandra Sequence*, will be published by Carcanet in August.

PADRAIG REGAN is currently working towards a PhD in the Seamus Heaney Centre for Poetry on the work of Anne Carson, and adaptation of medieval poetry. Padraig's poems have been published in *The Poetry Review, Ambit* and *Magma*. Padraig received an Eric Gregory Award in 2015.